A MORAL DISEASE

DELNO JONES

WestBow
PRESS
A DIVISION OF THOMAS NELSON

WestBow Press books may be ordered through booksellers or by contacting:

WestBow Press
A Division of Thomas Nelson
1663 Liberty Drive
Bloomington, IN 47403
www.westbowpress.com
1-(866) 928-1240

ISBN: 978-1-4497-3825-9 (sc)
ISBN: 978-1-4497-3824-2 (hc)
ISBN: 978-1-4497-3826-6 (e)

Library of Congress Control Number: 2012901274

Printed in the United States of America

WestBow Press rev. date: 2/29/2012

INTRODUCTION

MY STORY

At the age of fifteen I had begun to search for a place in life. Along about this time my parents had divorced; they were dealing with their own issues, feelings of rejection and new relationships. My brother and I were practically overlooked during this transition in all our lives, and I really took advantage of all this freedom.

In examining my past, I now realize I had an acceptance issue. Lacking parental and self discipline, my grades suffered. I couldn't compete with my more intelligent friends. I was an average athlete, not the best. I was popular enough in school, holding some class and club offices, but this wasn't enough. It seemed I always had to perform to receive the acceptance I needed. I was a people pleaser.

There was a group who had something confidential and mysterious going on. Not wanting to be left out of anything, I set out to find their secret. Their secret was alcohol and drugs. Alcohol didn't work for me. My behavior was performance oriented which led me to compete with more seasoned drinkers. I didn't like being out of control or fiercely sick for days afterwards. The drugs, on the other hand, worked in the beginning. They gave me courage to perform without the energy it took in the past. I thought I had discovered the solution for my insecurity.

After high school I went on to school in Atlanta. This was a true learning experience which included a few small encounters with law enforcement. Growing up in a small town like Cochran had its advantages. The officers at home gave us a lot of grace in hopes my friends and I were just growing up.

I came home after completing a two year struggle with being uncomfortable and feeling out of place. I was a country boy in the bright lights – too much exposure for my lifestyle. Returning home, I found my old crowd had turned legal age just like me. As we grew older, our behavior had become more dangerous and destructive.

I soon married in hopes of somewhat settling down. We quickly found ourselves in a dysfunctional relationship and pregnant. Our daughter was born in 1980, and we were divorced in less than a year. During the next eight years, I stayed somewhat grounded. Raising a daughter as a single father was a learning experience to say the least.

In 1988, I married my wife of twenty-two years now. Marrying Moni was the smartest thing I ever did in my life. She has taught me about honor, devotion and, most importantly, love. We had three wonderful children in the next seven years.

In 1983, I had two water skiing accidents in which I sustained neck and shoulder injuries. The repetitive nature of my work aggravated these injuries and caused me to be in constant pain. In 1994, I had met my demise – narcotic pain medication. I had my third surgery and a full blown addiction to the pills by 1999.

To recap several years here, let me just say I had seven surgeries, was in three secular drug rehabilitations and four detox facilities, had two walk out attempts when I didn't get my way, had one on one sessions with certified addiction counselors and attended countless AA and NA meetings. My life was miserable.

I found myself waking up angry all the time. I was so tired; it was almost too much of an effort to get through each day. I was emotionally and spiritually empty. I began to think dying would be easier, but, thankfully, I knew this would cause even more pain for my loved ones.

I finally realized I had tried every option to get better except God himself. I had such low self-esteem I didn't think I was even worthy of His love.

So, I had another meltdown and called for an intervention with my family. My wife, at this point, was emotionally bankrupt and had lost all compassion and hope for my recovery. Little did I know Moni had given up and turned me over to God.

My mom, brother and I began to once again search for yet another facility since it was out of the question I could stop this insanity on my own. During our search, I remembered my family doctor and friend had said to me, "You need to attempt recovery some other way, not yours." I had a moment of clarity and decided to try God's way.

I went to Tallulah Falls, Georgia, in an effort to find the God everyone said I needed. Here was the first time I ever heard "God is not lost, you are."

After a twenty week stay there, I had become healthy again. I was feeling better about myself and ready to conquer the world. The only issue was my family; were they ready for me? I thought if I was okay, they should be, too.

Graduation from Victory Home was one of the most exciting moments of my life – that is until Moni and my youngest son arrived alone. Everyone else was busy doing the things that were important to them. Obviously, they had heard all my apologies and promises before; they meant nothing any longer. Forced to be the man of the house, my oldest son, D. J., was working. Drew was there because he's the one who always tried to save me. Moni was there to give me a ride home.

When I asked where was Rayna, my wife said, "She said she didn't want to hear anything you had to say, she only wants to see you do something different." This was my real beginning of change.

When I returned home, I knew I had to make every effort to change; I couldn't do it without God's help. While changing every aspect of my old ways, I bounced around from church to church looking for the place most comfortable.

I ran into an old friend from school who asked if I'd be interested in teaching a recovery class at the local prison. I accepted, thinking I'd go and teach what I had learned. Little did I know this would be the beginning of my own growth and maturity.

In my past secular programs and meetings, we typically would choose a topic and discuss it. In the class in the prison, there were so many different people with incredible amounts of pain, uncontrollable emotions and troubled spirits it was impossible to stay on one topic.

This encouraged me to write about different emotions and behaviors. Since I have no training or degree on paper, I had to rely on experience. I soon realized all the past rehabs had contributed to my recovery in some capacity. Still, I had never written papers or essays. I had to write from my heart about my own thoughts and behavior.

In the process of writing and teaching, I had a lot of help and input from many people who believed in not only what I was doing but who believed in me. Then there was this phenomenon – I would begin writing but the words and thoughts weren't always mine. No doubt I held the pen but God was busy writing. Many nights after teaching at the prison, an inmate would ask how I knew she needed this. I didn't; God did!

With the encouragement of family, friends, pastors and all those who have loved and supported me, I have compiled my thoughts, ideas and experiences into this publication. This is an approach to recovery other than what I was taught at any one time.

Each time I returned home, I had a renewed spirit and good intentions, but this last time was different. I realized I had work to do. I could no longer be lazy, complacent or careless. There was no room in my life or the lives of my family for talk; it was time for action.

For the first time in recovery, I began to search diligently for the whys and whats that caused me to become addicted. Joey, a lifelong friend from childhood who has a psychology degree, made me realize it was my continuing to make bad choices. In discussions with Joey, the word "behavior" stood out most.

Most people believe if it wasn't for the alcohol and drugs and their consequences, I wouldn't be in this position. It has become apparent to me these weren't the problem. It was, has been and still is my behavior that's the culprit. With God's help, I can control my behavior.

I feel so blessed. God is leading me; I am following. It is my hope these writings might help answer questions and give guidance to those addicted and those in recovery and to their loved ones.

THANK YOU

I would like to take the time to thank all the people God has placed in my path and in the lives of my family during my recovery. It is such a long list that it has been a difficult decision to know who was most helpful. I asked my fifteen year old daughter Rayna what she thought I should do. After thinking, this was Rayna's reply:

> No one person has been more helpful than any other. It may seem so because some are upfront and talking to you directly, like the preacher. But don't forget those who prayed you through it; you'd be nowhere without them. You, also, don't want to forget the people who supported your family; we couldn't have done what we did without support from others. You, also, can't leave out financial supporters. Last, but not least, you can't forget the people that seemed not to have helped you at all, but in their on way they did. These are the people who showed you what you don't want to ever be again!

I would like to acknowledge the love, kindness, patience, and devotion my family has given me through the years. The trials have been long and tiring at times, but with God becoming the center of our lives there has been much joy in the journey. I have a tremendous amount of gratitude for every person who was there at each avenue I reached in my recovery.

It took each and everyone who believes in God's saving grace, mercy and redemption, the same ones who believed in me when I didn't believe in myself.

Thank you for your prayers and support.

Delno Jones.

TABLE OF CONTENTS

SERENITY PRAYER

God, grant me the serenity to accept the people who can not change,

Courage to change the one I can,

And the wisdom to know it's me.

ACCEPTANCE AND REJECTION

When I started writing about acceptance and rejection, I started thinking about the definitions. Accept is to receive, to admit; acceptance is reception. Reject is to cast off, to discard, to repel, to forsake, to decline. The Bible says to reject is to refuse (Romans 5:3).

Can we look at where we are now and accept (admit) that where we are today will help us grow? We need to examine where we are in our hearts and minds. How did we get here and where did it start? For scripture, turn to Romans 5:3. Know that we CAN RECOVER.

If our decline began with peer pressure/friends and we are still 'hanging' with these folks, we are still making bad choices. We have to acknowledge these people probably have some of the same behaviors we have to change in our own lives. Of course, these people will accept us back in their world. We make them feel better about their 'stuff' and/or they benefit from our inability to say, "no." We have to accept that we have to find new relationships.

Sometimes we are not accepted back in some of our circles. These people didn't 'use,' and they don't understand us. We have done things they don't seem to be able to forgive. We have to accept the responsibility for our wrongs, try to correct them and then make amends. That's all we can do for now.

Often times our behavior is rejected or refused as the Bible says. Many times it should be! It's been said rejection is a bitch! Such is life. Someone has hurt us - spouses, children, boyfriends, girlfriends, friends. We must examine these relationships and situations and, especially, our part in leading up to the rejection. How do we deal with the rejection? We find and build new healthy relationships.

How do we become accepted? Sometimes or in most cases, we start over. There is a story in the Bible of Jesus not performing any miracles in the town where he was born. The people knew Jesus as just a child and watched him grow up. They had doubts he was the one after whom they should mirror themselves. We often find it impossible to minister to others at home. These people know us, know our past; they don't believe in us, nor believe we can change.

There is the story in Luke 9 of the Samaritan woman who hemorrhaged for twelve years. This lady was ashamed because she was rejected by her people. She felt she was different; she isolated herself. There was a rumor Jesus was coming to town. She knew he could heal her if she could get close enough to touch him. (We know he can heal us if we can get close.) She went to town and found a crowd made up of Christians, much like those Christians who sit on the front row at church and think we can't be changed. She had to fight her way through the crowd. We as Christians sometimes get in God's way when we don't offer to be of service and help those in need.

The lady made it through all the shame, ridicule, fear and pain, never giving up and not caring about the possible consequences. She slipped up behind Jesus and touched the tassel on his robe. Jesus was on a mission to help another one of his children but stopped to say, "Who touched me? Someone in this crowd needs me and I'm here. Right now you are the most important to me because you believe I can heal you." The woman answered quietly, "It was I." Why did she answer quietly? The lady still didn't feel worthy because of the way the public had treated here, the way she was taught to feel. Jesus touched her and told her to go and be healed (Phil. 1:27).

Sometimes and in some cases we will not be accepted and will be rejected in our own hometowns. I talked to my wife about this. I can't minister to people at home because they don't believe in me. She said, "The example of what you were and what you are now is a ministry in itself."

ADDICTION

What is addiction? The word technically means the brain has become neurochemically dependent on a substance ingested into the body or on the chemicals the brain produces and releases when being involved in certain behaviors that create pleasure and excitement to that person. Research says the brain actually craves the substance or substance producing behavior in order to maintain the desired feeling. Over time it takes more and more of the substance to achieve the same effect. The brain adjusts and builds a high tolerance. When these chemicals are taken away, the mind and body go into withdrawal.

This says we use drugs to change the way we feel or use some kind of activity that gives the same pleasure to the brain. Then over time we begin to use more consistently until it stops working for us no matter how much we use or combine it with pleasure seeking behavior. Thoughts of certain behavior, such as fantasizing about sex, can cause intense feelings of pleasure. Gamblers, also, experience a release of adrenaline when taking risks and winning hands. Some of us have been so severely hurt in the past that we have to desensitize by using drugs to be intimate with another person. Many of us need intense therapy to recover.

Research has shown that very few addicts have only one addiction. One addiction may trigger another, or we may use one to gain the courage or to feel comfortable to do the other. Research has diagnosed and labeled this disorder as Multiple Addiction Disorder (MAD).

Whether we use chemicals or chemical producing behavior, our mind and body become addicted. Recovery is difficult when these two behaviors are compatible and enhance one another. A dependency is developed when we continually use drugs to seek relief from or for our emotions.

How did it happen? Is it loneliness? Starving for love? Many of us are angry because of or the lack of attention. Anger is usually an unwanted feeling. It doesn't matter from where our pain stems, we just don't want to feel it. Many of us as children were unable to form healthy attachments with our parents. This is another reason we form relationships with drugs. We are trying to obtain the calmness and warm fuzzy feeling as if mom was holding us. We spend a lot of time attempting to return to the womb where we were secure rather than putting forth the effort to grow and mature.

We, also, try to control our own lives and emotions; addiction has made us fail. "For what I am doing, I do not understand; for I am not practicing what I would like to do, but I am doing the very thing I hate" (Romans 7:15).

In active addiction, we create more pain which in turn creates more guilt and shame with which to handle and another scar on our self-esteem. These emotions, along with pain, chemicals and behavior, drive us deeper into addiction.

Sobriety or remaining in recovery takes a tremendous amount of spiritual, emotional and physical work. Spiritually, we must admit to our powerlessness while in active addiction. Most of us fear that admitting to being powerless shows weakness; our pride can very well hinder recovery.

Emotionally, we must search our hearts, identify our pain and forgive. Forgiveness is for our own well being. Sharing our pain, victories and defeats with our groups, counselors or accountability partners helps us let go; addiction loses it grip. We recognize our old attitudes and behaviors, then form new healthy habits.

Physically, the body is very resilient. Some may need to seek medical attention in the beginning. Specialized caregivers are in place for our health and safety to assist in recovery.

In our selfish, self-centered and impatient lives, we have wants and desires and know how to get instant gratification. We are fortunate to live in a time where science and culture provide the opportunity for recovery. Most of us have spiritual leaders who are testimonies to recovery. "Not by power, not by might, but by my spirit saith the Lord." Only God can change you and me. And let's not forget the battle is his, not ours.

"Watch out! Don't let me find you living in careless ease and drunkenness and filled with worries of this life. Don't let that day catch you unaware" (Luke 21:34).

"Don't you know that your body is a temple of the Holy Spirit, who lives in you and was given to you by God? You do not belong to yourself" (I Corinthians 6:19-20). God bought you with a high price; you must honor Him with your body.

"Don't be drunk with wine because that will ruin your life. Instead let the Holy Spirit fill and control you" (Ephesians 5:18).

"Without wavering, let us hold tightly to the hope we say we have, for God can be trusted to keep his promise. Think of ways to encourage one another to outbursts of love and good deeds. And let us not neglect our meeting together, as some people do, but encourage and warn each other , especially now that the day of his coming is near" (Hebrews 10:23-25).

AGAINST NOTHING

When we begin in recovery, the majority of us think we have to hate alcohol and drugs. Most of us and people in general think chemicals are our only problem.

We tend to develop an attitude of indifference towards our recovery programs and the people in them. We attempt to discredit and find anything and everything wrong with the very principles which will lead us to a happy and healthy life in recovery.

In active addiction we have no discipline and have little in the beginning of sobriety. We are rebellious to the point we are not tolerant to authority in the process of recovery. We are angry when someone calls our attention to our "stinking thinking" or our working another person's program and avoiding looking at our own mess.

In our addiction when the drugs actually started working against us, our lives became unmanageable; we lost sight of all emotional, mental and spiritual health. In turn our thinking is negative, full of hate, mad with the world and most of the people in it. Our problems are always someone else's fault.

Many times when we form first impressions of someone, we tend to pick out all their flaws. We compare their downfalls to ours in hopes their problems will be more dysfunctional, so we can feel better about ourselves.

There are many conflicts in the lives of addicts and alcoholics, those in and out of recovery. It often seems the world is against us.

We learn in recovery that certain people, places and things are forbidden, especially drugs and alcohol. Our arrogance tells us we are more intelligent, we can beat the system. We just don't like being told what to do and how to live our lives.

After a brief time of being clean, we think we are sober. The result of being rid of the drugs but still having the bad attitude, quick to anger is called a "dry drunk." The absence of drugs and alcohol alone cannot be considered being in sobriety.

We hear so many "don'ts and can'ts" our mindset becomes very negative. In scripture, God wrote ten commandments. The Pharisees added 623 more don'ts and can'ts. We perceive life as all the things we can not and should not do. We think we are supposed to hate sin and anyone who sins.

During our upbringing, we were taught the things we should be against, such as lying, cheating, stealing, doing drugs and alcohol, etc. So many times we forget the importance of love. Scripture doesn't say we should hate; it says we should turn away from things which are not pleasing to God.

If we are not careful in recovery, we will spend all our time trying to avoid the don'ts. We will not have the time or energy to recognize the good and positive aspects in our lives. We should pay attention and count all our small blessings. We need to focus on details we may not think are important. Missing small details in recovery can add up to huge mistakes.

There needs to be balance in recovery. If we focus too much on the walk, we lose the joy in the journey!

Here's an analogy from the book of Moni, my wife. If you take a dirty pot and put forth your best efforts in cleaning it, getting rid of all the grime, eventually you will have a clean but empty pot. If you take that dirty pot and continue running clean water in it, the pot will become clean and filled with pure water.

If we focus on just cleaning ourselves up, getting rid of the drugs without cleaning up our attitudes, we will miss the joy God intended for us. Our emptiness will be the breeding ground for destruction.

Scripture says when an evil spirit leaves a person, it goes to the desert looking for rest but finds none. It returns to the house and finds it clean but empty. It goes back and returns with seven spirits even more evil; they take up residence in the house. That person is then worse off than ever.

Cleaning out our house is first and foremost of importance. Filling our house with God, family and healthy relationships will guarantee evil can not enter.

A great friend, pastor and songwriter has a song that goes something like this: Don't forget to smell the roses. You have time so take it; don't hurry. It isn't about the destination. It will always be there waiting. What you want to remember most at the end of the road is the journey.

ANGER

Anger is an emotion. When it is followed by the wrong action or reaction, it usually becomes aggressive. Aggressive anger can cause threatening situations and usually progresses into hostile situations. This is normal behavior for us who have to have a defense in place for the actions or behavior we display.

Anger, when held back or not dealt with immediately, becomes resentment. It sits there and smolders and festers; soon this anger will seek revenge. Anger can, also, cause physical problems such as headaches and stomach problems, all of which we do not want to feel. These feelings and emotions, if handled in the wrong way, can be a trigger.

We can hold resentment for a long time. We have all heard statements such as these: "You will never amount to anything. You're no good. Why can't you be more like your brother/sister?" Statements like this hurt. These are coming from loved ones, people for whom we care. These hurt feelings turn into resentment.

Remarks from the general public are usually followed by guilt and shame. Then this guilt and shame turns into anger and resentment.

Lots of times people say these hurtful things as their own defense from being hurt and disappointed themselves. Another way to look at it would be, could they be coming short of their expectations of you or not wanting to acknowledge their own failures?

Every time I think of the hurt I have caused, I have one more reason to 'use.'

I can't physically do anything about it or emotionally express my feelings without a bad reaction. So I just hold the feelings in; they grow and one more time I try to use non-human intervention for a human problem in an attempt to kill the pain.

If channeled in the right way, anger can be positive. When we get tired of being tired and downright mad with our disease, we are able to use our anger to fight and stop addiction from controlling us.

"Be angry, and yet do not sin; do not let the sun go down on your anger, and do not give the devil an opportunity" (Ephesians 4:26-27).

"A God ready to pardon, gracious and merciful, slow to anger, and of great kindness" (Nehemiah 9:17).

We should attempt to be open, honest and communicate responsibly with people who hurt, use and make us angry. The end result will not become a sensitive wound in our hearts and minds.

In the end of these struggles, there has to be forgiveness. We have to ask forgiveness for the things we have put our loved ones through, and we have to forgive others. This is imperative for our recovery. Forgiveness is for you.

Mark 11:24-25 says, "If and when you pray, and you believe you have them, they will be given to you. But first you must forgive anyone you have anything against before Jesus Christ will forgive your sins too."

ANGER MANAGEMENT

It has been said that ten seconds acted out in anger or rage can change the next ten years of one's life. And not in a good way!

We all need to learn to control our anger. We can go it alone, using self will and self control. We learn to recognize what triggers our anger, staying out of situations where we would be tempted to anger. Or we can seek God's help.

The best anger management of all comes from a spiritual experience or awakening through Christ. An experience can happen all at once; the anger and rage we feel can just leave us. God can do that; He can remove that anger.

An awakening comes from maturity only to be found by following God's words and principles. Maturity in Christ produces the fruit of the spirit; that spirit lives within us. Galatians 5:22 says, "But the fruit of the spirit is love, joy, peace, patience, kindness, goodness, faithfulness, gentleness and self control."

When we live by the spirit, we learn to have love for people just as they are, have patience with them and have self control. All this works in our favor.

For a number of years, there has been a popular bracelet with the letters W W J D. These letters stands for "what would Jesus do?" The next time we feel anger, we need to stop and think W W J D.

ANXIOUS

Webster defines anxious as characterized by extreme uneasiness of mind or brooding fear about some contingency; worrying; ardently wishing or eager. Anxiety is painful or apprehensive uneasiness of mind; fearful concern or interest.

There is a quote from the book The Shack by Young: "We rarely live in the present, we relive the past, worrying (anxious) about the future."

Being anxious is uncomfortable; we cannot rest or relax properly. Normally this results from fear, being shamed or humiliated, and we worry about being accepted. There is usually a cost for being anxious. We get in a hurry and forget important steps or even avoid valuable areas of recovery.

Be careful! Addictive behavior says, "We want what we want and we want it now." The pace can be too fast. Running constantly, whether it is consciously or unconsciously, will seem as familiar as an adrenaline rush, physically creating a panic if it continues. It didn't happen in one day, give it time.

Fear of the unknown plays a huge part. Fear itself is a natural and necessary emotion given to us by God as a defense. It is, also, physical. That is why when we get anxious we feel nervous and tense; our heart rate increases and we sweat at times.

Worry is a companion of being anxious. Wasted energy! Worry is not an emotion but a thought or thoughts that lead to anxiety. Stinkin' thinkin' is an unhealthy and unreasonable mindset which attempts to solve situations out of our control. Instead of stopping, being still, thinking and praying to let things go that cannot be controlled, we get anxious and obsess over controlling the problem and worrying about how bad things are and how terrible the results will be if the problem is not solved right away.

While in recovery, if the character of our behavior does not change, it will not appear to anyone that we have changed. We often talk about how our families have the need to recover; they need to recover from our behavior. Being too anxious interferes with our ability to wait on delayed gratification. Having expectations of others, constantly hurrying them with our obsessions and compulsions to fix, get started, finish, etc. looks like our suspicious past – the past when we were always anxious about getting the money, finding the drugs and hurrying to the place to use them. Being anxious causes us to do things we may regret. When we are too aggressive for people and they fail to respond in a manner suitable to us, we get angry and bitter and then develop new unfair resentments. Our desperation has put too many expectations on ourselves and others.

Anxious worry is pointless and unable to solve problems. No anxious thought about tomorrow will bring success to recovery today. Anxious worry is a pattern of thinking that 'controls' people who try to live independent of God. Anxiety and its companion worry, which is Satan, constantly try to separate us from God.

We get caught up in worrying about the future and about things that haven't happened yet. Anxiety makes us afraid that no one understands how significant our circumstances are to us. So therefore, we lose focus on the One who tells us, "Be anxious for nothing."

When we are able to give our anxiety to God, He replaces it with a "peace that surpasses all understanding." When we begin to feel anxious, we should hit our knees in prayer. He will give us the peace he promised.

"Be anxious for nothing, but in everything by prayer and supplication, with thanksgiving, let your requests be made to God; and the peace of God, which surpasses all understanding, will guard your hearts and minds through Christ Jesus" (Philippians 4:6-7).

John 14:1 says, "Let not your heart be troubled."

Now there is a positive view of 'anxious.' Always be anxious to share the gospel! Always be anxious to tell people what Jesus has done for you!

As a supplement to my thoughts on being anxious, I'd like to share with you thoughts from my family. I asked my wife to explain to me what anxious meant to her. She said living with me in active addiction was constantly a worry; she was always anxious, never knowing what was next. She was always uneasy when the phone rang, answering with a fear of who and what she would hear. She feared I was calling to say I had a meltdown and was going to rehab or someone was calling to say I was dead. If I was on the way home, she never knew in what condition I would be or what my attitude would be. She was just always anxious to get it over with. She would be so anxious, she couldn't focus on small tasks. Family events were always important to her, but let her try to get an outing or anything else together. Everything was always up in the air, what time will we leave or will we even go. The only thing she had constant in her life was prayer and the only thing she could hold onto was her belief in God. Every morning her prayer would be that today would be the day I would change.

My mother's husband said the mailman, with his infinite wisdom, often helps him. He said the opposite of anxious is patient. Good things come to those who are patient!

ARROGANT AND UNTEACHABLE

In my journey to recovery, I visited several treatment centers and frequented a couple and had many failed attempts trying to get sober on my own. I once participated in a group meeting facilitated by a CAC, Certified Addiction Counselor, and had one on one sessions in which he was compensated by the hour. While under his care, my addiction told me I could go to all these meetings and people would think I was doing really well, especially if I knew all the right answers and said the things people wanted to hear. Somewhere along the way, I began feeling better about myself, my mind was clearing up somewhat and I was getting healthy again. So I started thinking I've got this! I've learned everything I need to know. I can preach it! I can teach it!

Just when I decided to impress everyone with my brilliance, my counselor, suddenly and in a confrontational manner, called me arrogant and unteachable. I thought this was merely because I had challenged his knowledge about addictive behavior. Of course, this made me very angry. For about two years, I thought the audacity of a man who is so arrogant himself to say he is never wrong to call anybody else arrogant. I had thoughts of many ways to hurt this man and had turned my attention to him instead of my own recovery. As time passed and even today, I know how right he was. Too, I know his job was to build me up and make me think differently about myself. I needed to realize I was not a bad person, just one who had made a lot of bad choices.

When we get built up, sometimes we forget who the teacher is and we become unteachable. We begin to think you don't know me, I'm different. We get self-righteous and get the idea we are not as bad as the next addict. We are very stubborn in turning away from our addictive thinking. We begin to have an 'attitude' when someone points out our shortcomings and our personality and character defects. We become arrogant and think we know what is best. I'm going to do it my way! When we are not open to suggestions and new ideas and are unwilling to see them as beneficial instead of seeing everything as criticism, we are unteachable.

After we become comfortably miserable, there is a time in recovery when we decide maybe someone knows more than I do. I'll start listening instead of trying to teach, hearing instead of talking, taking the cotton out of my ears and sticking it in my mouth. I've decided to try to be humble, but then I'm still strong willed and have pride. My pride says I'm not powerless. I then fight through my pride issue, and I have this self-esteem complex. I have hurt so many people in my past and have painfully come this far in recovery that I want to impress everyone around me with my new way of creative thinking that I forget about recovery itself and catch myself not applying the principles to my life. During this whole recovery process, I obtained much knowledge but was still talking the talk but not walking the walk.

I have an 80 year old friend Mrs. Johnnie. You may think at her age, she wouldn't understand what we are talking about, but she always teaches me when I listen. She quoted a proverb in this way, "Knowledge without wisdom makes a fool."

Proverbs 1:7 says, "Fear of the Lord is the beginning of knowledge. Only fools despise wisdom and discipline." Without the wisdom to use knowledge, I am a fool. I must let go of my pride, get out of my own self-will and ask God to be my teacher and reveal to me the knowledge he would have me to need. I was once told, "Don't be discouraged if you feel like your knowledge is little. Just exercise the wisdom you do have."

Read the first five chapters of Proverbs.

ATTITUDES

Our attitudes are a reflection of our inner selves. Attitudes, also, affect the first impressions others have of us and the way we see and judge the character of others. Our attitudes are transitional, the way we feel when we wake up in the morning, the way we perceive our self-worth, what we think others think of us. Be careful not to value self-worth from past behavior, because here we develop an attitude of self pity.

Our attitudes change by our circumstances, but our circumstances should not determine our actions. Some of us have a pessimistic attitude, thinking nothing ever works in our favor and always expecting the worst. An optimistic attitude always tries to see good in everything and brings hope. A negative attitude breeds destructive behavior. With a negative attitude, we have no hope and usually will not accept positive advice or suggestions.

When bad things happen to us, instead of the attitude of why did this happen to me, just maybe we should ask what should I be able to learn from this. With a positive attitude, nothing is as bad as it seems; it allows us to see the good in everything.

Many of us have an attitude of indifference. We just don't care. Argumentative people thrive on being right and try to justify their behavior. The most critical attitude for me is the rebellious attitude. Rules are made to be broken; I can get forgiveness easier than I can get permission. I continue to hurt those I love by doing it my way. This leads to a self-centered attitude. No matter who or how bad it hurts, it's all about me.

We have feelings we have no control over; we have temptations in our thoughts that are beyond our control. But attitude is a behavior all of us can control. If I don't change my attitude, not a whole lot changes. My Dad says, "Attitude is a condition of the heart," whether you are warm or cold hearted, tender or hard hearted.

We must become entirely ready for God to remove our character defects. It seems impossible to remove all. It is humanly impossible to reach perfection. God desires to have us perfect, but He does accept progress. "Those who become Christians become new creatures. They are not the same anymore, for the old has past and the new life has begun (2 Corinthians 5:17).

Yet I still have bad days; I get irritable and angry, and my attitude is terrible. "I know I'm rotten through and through as far as my sinful nature is concerned. No matter which way I turn. I can't make myself right. I want to, but I can't. When I want to do good, I don't. And when I try not to do wrong, I do it anyway. But if I am doing what I don't want to do, I am not really the one doing it, it's the sin in me (Romans 7:18-20).

When we have a positive attitude and make a conscious effort, when we participate with God and accept the guidance he freely gives, our attitudes and perspective on life changes. Our life changes for the better.

Philippians 3:12 says, "I don't mean to say that I have already achieved these things or that I have already reached perfection. But I keep working toward that day when I will be all that Christ Jesus saved me for and wants me to be."

BALANCE IN RECOVERY

In active addiction, our attention is focused on one thing and one thing only – how and where to find the drugs. We don't have the time for anyone or anything else. Everyone and everything else becomes secondary to our addiction.

Now we want to change, and we find ourselves in recovery. Our whole focus has to be on recovery. We are taught by the secular programs to be selfish in our recovery, to do 90 in 90, ninety meetings in ninety days. The ones who have intentions of recovering from addiction tend to eat, sleep, breathe, make the coffee and talk it constantly. That's a good thing, because the fact is, if we didn't, our characters will have us repeating our previous behavior.

Our previous lifestyles had no structure. Structure is important in recovery. In the beginning, recovery has to be very specific about how we should do things. Structure has steps; we do things repeatedly and at specific times. This structure can be so regimented we get confused and troubled when a change of plans or conflicts arise.

As time passes, hopefully, we will develop some stability in our mental and emotional growth and maturity. We no longer want to be addicts with addiction dictating the rest of our lives. Yet we become distraught thinking about having to live such strict and structured programmed lifestyles in recovery. If we remain in the program, we will hear the word "balance" and learn what it is.

A balance is our time spent proportionally between relationships, work and relaxation. We will get to a place where the struggling with the mental obsessions of using has passed, and we become comfortable in our perspective recovery groups, churches, Bible studies or whatever has replaced our addiction.

In attempting to keep everything in harmony and proportion, we will run into conflicts and circumstances we can not control. Things arise that are beyond our control. We must be able to adjust our agendas.

When we are more tolerant to change and can put others' needs ahead of our own selfish needs, we are learning balance. Selfishness is pointed out here to remind us that we can put others ahead of ourselves. We no longer have to be so rigid in our recovery. We are learning balance.

I give you the analogy of an oak tree. An oak tree is a strong hard wood but can be brittle in dry times. A wind or storm comes along, and the oak can crack under the stress. Like the oak if we are so rigid, we, too, can crack.

It may not be evident why God wasn't mentioned in the balance. If we consider when we are God's followers, we will always try to be aware of how He does things. When we faithfully keep Him in our hearts and minds, we begin to develop His character. It becomes evident in us, and His behavior will continually occur and reoccur in our walk to recovery. God is always in the balance.

BOREDOM

Boredom can be what initiates the curiosity we had about drugs. Boredom can be a very dangerous condition. Being idle or becoming complacent causes us to get careless in recovery and life in general.

Before we began our journey into addiction, we sat around or isolated ourselves and denied ourselves the availability of relationships with people. We did not take advantage of any resources offered to us to be an active part of society.

There is the fact that a greater percentage of addicts are above average in intelligence which creates the capacity to get bored with everyday life. The intelligent mind often gets worn out with repetition. This is the reason why recovery without a purpose usually fails. If we always have intentions and fail to follow through, continually avoid the work, don't put forth the energy, don't engage or have a lack of interest, this could be due to just plain laziness. After a while we become weary, our patience wears thin, we have little tolerance and cannot imagine how we will ever find ourselves or pleasure again. When we do have an interest in something, we can't focus. We have trouble finding direction and have feeling of uselessness.

Boredom is a breeding ground for destruction. We get to a point where our spirits are so low, we fall into depression. This creates a feeling of dejection and sadness followed by a difficulty in thinking and concentration. By now, in this frame of mind, we are easily manipulated and convinced to do things we know we should not do and normally would not do. We justify it by saying we are tired of fighting. Actually our inactivity has not fought at all. Boredom is a worthless motivation, a useless activity followed by sadness, hollow feelings and broken spirits.

When we begin our adventure into recovery, the program teaches us we have to avoid old habits, people, places and things. We attempt to sit back, like we are taught, and be still during trying times; all that happens is we see the reflection of our past. The pain in our lives flashes repeatedly in our minds. The drugs that we had discovered worked in the beginning by primarily killing that pain. With the knowledge we possess and the low self-esteem we have, there is an acceptance problem. We used drugs to be accepted. Now it seems we are pressured into using once again to perform.

Instead of changing our circle of friends, we hesitate getting involved with new people for fear of not fitting in. The new people and ideas are just not appealing. For so long our courage was artificial and gave us a false sense of security. In the end this worked against us; it became paranoid insecurity. Without that crutch, we got bad attitudes. Then we were overtaken by enough feelings of desperation to seek instant gratification. Boredom is a behavior in which we can not afford to participate.

There is a very real occurrence many of us have experienced in relapse. We are taught in recovery that addiction is progressive. This means two things: "As our use continues, we become immune to the drugs and our dependency requires more and more. While in recovery, we do not have the luxury of starting over from the beginning. Our addiction is still alive and well." We relapse and pick up where we left off.

Scripture says in Matthew 12:43-45, "When an evil spirit leaves a person, it goes to the desert looking for rest, and when it finds none, it goes back to the house, finding it clean and empty. It goes out and finds seven spirits even more evil than itself and they come back and live there." That person is worse off than when he began.

This is speaking biblically of the progression of relapse. We get cleaned up and fail to fill our house with the Holy Spirit, and relapse is inevitable. Some of us think we can do it once, and we will always have protection. We have to continually keep ourselves full of God's love. Many of us try every possible way to be successful at recovery. Filling our house with anything but the freedom that comes from God can not guarantee to keep out demons.

"Come to me all who are weary and heavy laden and I will give you rest" (Matthew 11:28). Rest means settled (comfort), tranquility (peace), and refreshed spirit.

Rest is God's gift to us for being still and quiet without being bored. I can finally feel at ease alone.

BOUND UP

What is in our past or better yet our behavior that keeps us bound up? Whatever it is, it has such a strong hold on us that we continue to make wrong choices and use the same methods to change the way we feel. There are many incidences in our past we regret and of which we feel guilty and ashamed. Addiction has this not so funny way of compiling this guilt; the more drugs we use in order to avoid feeling guilt, the more guilt we feel.

Guilt is a painful emotion that gives us the ability to reason between right and wrong. This gives guilt both positive and negative aspects. When we feel guilt, we should take it as a warning sign that our actions can stop before we go any further with bad choices. Pain, for most of us, is why we used in the beginning. We have lived with it for so long, and the drugs are the only solution we know.

The problem now is we have killed our emotions so many times it has become easier to avoid the warnings and just deal with the consequences. Many of us cannot conceive of how to begin to change. That is why we normally ignore the guilt, deny we have it and run away from it rather than facing up to it.

Once we have hurt someone, there is no amount of service or buying back with guilt gifts that works. The only thing that can show our remorse and will be adequate enough to relieve the person we hurt and ourselves is asking forgiveness.

The program tells us to make amends when possible. Sometimes

24

we cannot go to that particular person; we have to depend on other resources available to us, such as friends, counselors, sponsors, accountability partners, etc. These people usually understand, are not surprised and will not condemn us. These are our conventional solutions of making amends.

Personally admitting our wrongs and getting honest with someone we've hurt, unleashes the stronghold guilt has on us. Telling someone not only frees us but, also, gives them the confidence to know there is at least an attempt to change on our part. It, also, verifies what they probably already knew.

Just admitting our wrongs does not help us unless we change our behavior. The more we share our guilt the less significant the guilt becomes, and eventually it has no effect on us. If we continue to just say I'm sorry, it tends to have no effect on others.

When we discover we are not alone in recovery and trust someone with all our guilt and shortcomings, we then can tell our stories in their entirety – the good, the bad, the ugly, the indifference. Our shame then no longer has control over us. We can show ourselves as open books, candidly and frankly admitting our failures, not downplaying them, and commit to addressing the core issues that cause our behavior. These core issues are the thoughts and feelings we harbor. It feels good to tell our stories rather than having them thrown in our faces. When we become completely honest, it rids us of the guilt and shame, gives us a release from the bondage that oppresses and restrains us from recovery. Finally we can make a pledge to ourselves and others to live a life of service and quality, free from addiction, with the boldness to pursue our responsibilities.

Do not ignore the positive aspects of guilt. We know from our past the more guilt and shame there is, the greater the possibility of that vicious cycle of relapse and active addiction. We must use our guilt in a positive way. We can go to the Scriptures to know and seek guidance.

Romans 3:23 says, "All have fallen short of the glory of God."

In 2 Samuel 1-2, David, after becoming king, committed adultery and murder; he ignored it for a year. When he was confronted by the prophet Nathan, he finally confessed. After confessing David wrote Psalm 51: 1-19. Remembering God's mercy and love, he knew his prayer of forgiveness was sufficient. David admitted his sins to our ever forgiving God; he admitted all his thoughts, feelings and sinful actions. God then cleansed him and purified his heart. He then gave his word to God he would live by the Word and reap the benefits of living in unity rather than fighting against Him.

CARELESS

There is a time in our recovery, just after we become complacent that we have been disconnected and have allowed ourselves to get careless. We know we shouldn't do certain things, go to specific places and be around old acquaintances with dangerous behavior. Yet, we still have our arrogance and feel the need or desire to test our strength. None of us want to admit to ourselves we are weak. We think, even after countless failed attempts at sobriety, that we are stronger than the temptation. When we get careless and say, "To hell with all I know about myself and recovery," our actions will progressively lead us back to relapse and possibly back to full blown addiction.

There are several stages to addictive behavior. The first stage is preoccupation. This is where our mind becomes preoccupied with the beginning of our addiction. This is when the drugs and alcohol actually worked for us. The idea behind this is at first the drugs worked for our pain; at some point they stopped working; then shortly afterwards they begin to work against us. Preoccupation is more commonly referred to as obsessing over thoughts or temptations.

Stage two is ritualization. Rituals are those things we do such as driving down a too familiar street just to look around, stopping at a convenience store where alcohol is sold, buying a pack of cigarettes and a lighter from the same rack seen many times before, holding a cigarette in our mouth with no smoking habit and no intention of lighting it. All these things trigger feelings of excitement, nervousness, fear and anxiety which are dangerous emotions caused by carelessness.

Our nonchalant stroll down memory lane has turned into a serious trip.

Stage three is acting out, better known to us as craving. "One is too many and a thousand is never enough." We decide we are strong enough for just one. There we go, off to the races.

Stage four is the guilt and shame. If the guilt alone had been enough during the first and second stages, we as addicted people could resist the temptation. Sadly, it's not. We act out of our arrogance and/or stupidity. We are too lazy to address our addictive behavior. This behavior will not stop until the activities that lead up to it are exposed and eliminated. When we identify the behavior, we must share our rituals with accountability partners and our plan to avoid these rituals. Honesty is the key to a successful accountability.

Strengths in one area will not make us immune to temptation in another. Being careless and flirting with temptation allows failure in our recovery.

Read Judges 16 for the story of Sampson and Delilah. Sampson was the strongest man in the Bible; he failed because of his weakness to temptation.

No matter how bad things get, let your last thought be in prayer to God.

CHANGE

In our world today for the content and productive members of society, change is constant. In addiction and in our efforts to change the way we feel, time stops and change just does not exist as far as growth is concerned. Clinical studies show that maturity stops when we start using.

If we don't change the way we think and the way we do things, nothing ever changes. Thinking we can change from one drug to another is bad thinking and almost always leads to failure in sobriety. Any substance we use that changes the way we feel changes our focus, and our bodies then crave our new drug of choice. When I use, all I can think of is using more.

Real change takes time. Change doesn't occur in one day, so easy does it! So what do we do? Get out of seeking self-satisfaction and think of others first. We are not talking about changing the faults of others but changing ourselves in order to help people struggling with the same behavior. We don't have to be perfect to encourage others. We don't have to try to have all the answers; we just need to apply the wisdom we have.

How do we know we have changed? When we respond to people with a kind voice and a thoughtful heart, we realize our attitudes have changed. When we react to situations with calmness instead of defensively, we know we have changed.

How do others know we have changed? We often try hard to

please people with unusual acts of kindness to show our change or to get confirmation that they approve of our change. When change is real, we won't have to tell or show anyone; it will be evident.

Change can not occur on our own strength alone. We often say, "OK, I need to change my ways." 'I' alone almost always fail. 'I' alone lack enough will power. 'I' need help to change my ways.

We cannot change without the support of good healthy relationships. We need to develop and nurture the relationships of those who want to help us. We need to respect their suggestions, accept their support and emulate their examples.

To change is to be trained in a different way of thinking and living. We learn new ways to live and practice accountability for ourselves and others going through the same struggles. We must have a desire to mature and to possess healthy behavior.

We have to practice and discipline ourselves to acquire spiritual growth. Inner strength in us, alone, is not enough. Renewing of the mind and changing the way we think can not be accomplished alone. 2 Corinthians 5:17 says, "Therefore if anyone is in Christ, he is a new creation; old things have passed away; behold, all things have become new."

Change leads to growth. Growth leads to maturity. Maturity leads to change. God desires perfection but accepts change.

CHAOS

Chaos is where God does not go. Chaos is where God is not present. Chaos does not let God exist.

In active addiction, our lives have become chaotic. We create it; we live it. My wife says, "Living with an addict is total confusion, never knowing how you're going to be when you walk in the door, your attitude, your mental state, your emotional state. I'm always wondering what's next, what to do, what to say, will it be right or wrong. Plans are always up in the air. I can't count on you."

Chaos always looks for us, or is that just our perception? We have lived with it so long that chaos itself has become an addiction. If I see someone doing wrong, hear someone saying something I perceive as wrong or catch someone breaking rules, I love to take all that out of context and create chaos out of it. Sometimes I may think it's the right thing to do until I'm caught at my own game. Then I get defensive and even vindictive. We all have these chaotic excuses why it's not our fault. I've become good enough at turning things around and making it someone else's fault that often times he/she thinks it really is his/her fault.

Our attitudes change daily depending on the chaos that's around us. Granted it's usually us creating the chaos. We go to those places we shouldn't go and see those people we should avoid. It's our own doing that puts us in the position of being in the wrong place at the wrong time.

As we begin to recover, we can recognize chaos when it starts, or even before it starts. Take yourself out of that situation!

We can be recovering addicts, not using drugs, and still create chaos around us. We look at others, taking inventory, finding faults in them and sharing our findings with anyone who will listen. This keeps us from looking at ourselves; it, also, creates chaos so no one will look at us too closely. We continue to be miserable and make those around us miserable with our same old behavior.

Or we can be recovering Christians, taking personal inventory of our own lives. We need to ask God to help us with our shortcomings. We must have the knowledge to know when we are wrong and correct it without chaos. Recovering Christians should not worry, should trust and delight in His presence, commit their way, rest and wait patiently (Psalms 37). God stands just outside of chaos, waiting to pull us out.

We as recovering Christians should always look at how we can help, not hurt, others. We should look at how we can help build God's kingdom.

Remember if there is not change in our behavior, we are just dry drunks. We'll never be free from the bondage of misery.

CHOICES

What kind of choices do we have? We have right choices and we have wrong choices. We've all heard the line, when you get to the fork in the road, which way will you choose?

Now, we're faced with the choice to make a life changing decision. We make the wrong choice, and our excuse is I was in the wrong place at the wrong time. Bad luck, huh? There's no such thing as luck at this point. We could have turned and walked away.

Bad choices always cause consequences with which we must deal. These consequences have caused us time and time again to look at our behavior and seek help. Through medicine and psychiatry, we sometimes find some degree of relief. Often times, we're left clean but confused and exhausted.

We're still faced with choices. My Dad says, "To keep going in the same direction is the easy road." Do we repeat our same old behavior? We do have a choice at this junction in our lives.

We all know when we are clean it's often times a fight to stay that way. It's at one of those times we make the bad choice and use again. Addiction takes over; we lose control, our ability to choose and our option to stop. We continue to use until our drug causes so much pain we, again, have to ask for help. We say to ourselves, "How did I end up here, again? I must be insane to do this over and over."

We have the choice to change. It's easier to have the same thought pattern and make the same mistakes instead of trying to change. My friend Steve says, "We suffer more in recovery than we do when we're using because recovery requires change."

We all have a sinful nature; we have the temptation to do the wrong thing, make the wrong choice. Every step in life is a choice. When our lives have become miserable and unmanageable, we do have the choice to CHANGE.

Along with learned behavior, we need the help of others. We should seek and find good healthy relationships to help each other through the transition. We find a lot of our recovery is in sharing our hopes, strengths, experiences and needs in order to change and make good choices.

We have the choice to be honest with people and with ourselves. This leads to one of our most important moral choices. Do I choose to hurt or honor those who love and support me? Our greatest choice is whether we will choose to follow God or follow our own will. Normally, our will does not line up with God's plan and usually edifies Satan.

God's words about our will are found in Isaiah 66:4. "I will send great troubles against them – all troubles they feared. For when I called, they did not answer. When I spoke, they did not listen. They deliberately sinned – before my very eyes – and chose to do what they know I despise."

Read 1 Corinthians 1:26-28. "Remember that few of you were wise in the world's eyes, or powerful or wealthy when God called you. Instead, God deliberately chose things the world considers foolish in order to shame those who think they are wise. And he chose those who are powerless to shame those who are powerful. God choose those things despised by the world, things counted as nothing at all and used them to bring nothing what the world considers important." In verse 30 Jesus gave himself to make it a choice for us to be free. In freedom comes joy, peace, contentment and happiness.

It's not hard to be a God follower. Remember W. W. J. D. (What Would Jesus Do)! God gives us the same choices to be loving, kind, and patient to all people and to do the next right thing.

I have this choice. We all have this choice. My choice is to follow God's word. Jesus Christ will help me make good choices.

CODEPENDENCY

Codependency is when someone is dependent on another person's behavior. It could be a relative, spouse or caretaker. How does someone become codependent? Take these two scenarios. One case is by being a natural people pleaser. These people earn praise by performing acts of kindness, but they have a need to have these acts acknowledged publicly. They need this acknowledgment for their own self-worth.

Other codependents don't seem to begin this way. Codependency is sometimes forced on them by us. We as addicts have a lack of self-control; we can't take care of our families and business affairs. The people who love and care for us take responsibility and develop this way of life.

By continually enabling again and again, the codependent person gains control; the addict lets it happen and manipulates the person into thinking it's his/her idea. The codependent person sometimes encourages the addict's behavior in order to keep the control.

They want us to change, but only change the destructive behavior that would place us in jails or institutions or cause our death. They want us to change only the things that would cause us to be taken away from them. They would like us to give up destructive habits such as lying, cheating and stealing but not necessarily stop using because they may then loose control.

When we get sober and the codependent begins to loose control, he/she can be as deceiving and manipulative as the addict.

Of course, he/she learned from the best; all is fair in love and war! The codependent will at times jeopardize our sobriety in order to retain control. The codependent always makes it seem as if everything he/she does is in our best interest. When we change, the codependent is threatened once again that he/she may loose us and fails to realize that he/she has become as sick as the addict and needs recovery, too.

My mom is codependent. It started with her parents working on the farm and giving her responsibility in the kitchen. She received much praise for her good work. Then my father traveled in his work, and, again, my mom had to take charge of the home. As time passed and my father stopped traveling, Mom lost her control. My parents divorced, and my codependent mother married someone who was happy to let her take care of him and the home. We recognize her behavior as learned codependent behavior.

When I came home from rehab the eleventh time, things had to change. One day at work (oh, I've worked along side my mom for thirty years), she said, "This is the way we've always done things." There was no harm meant by that statement; it's just she never realized that to be part of my recovery, she would have to do things differently. She wanted everything to be back to normal, but my behavior and emotions were never normal.

At some point the codependent has to relinquish control. As you would know learned behavior begins to look considerably familiar to addiction itself. Whatever it takes to get his/her fix! In order to retain his/her status and control, the codependent may not tell the truth or may conjure things up in his/her mind until he/she believes it to be the truth. This is downright deceitful, yet the codependent may not even realize what he/she is doing or believe this is for our best.

We as addicts have to be very aware and careful to recognize codependence in others. The codependent may need us to be dysfunctional to some degree. We do not need dysfunction in our lives. We must be careful not to get careless and try to salvage some of our less destructive behaviors.

"When I want to do good, evil is right there with me. For in my inner beauty I delight in God's law. But I see another law at work in the members of my body, waging war against the law of my mind and making me a prisoner of the law of sin at work within my members" (Romans 7:21-23).

COMMIT

Commit means to entrust or practice. What is in us that prevents us from committing to do the right thing? We don't get involved in new and healthy activities. We don't commit to meetings, if not Narcotics Anonymous then some other recovery program, such as Overcomer's Outreach or Celebrate Recovery. We don't do anything but sit around until our minds tell us we've got it this time. We haven't worked a fourth step and got rid of the past; it sits there with us and grows until there is more pain than we can bear.

Why can't we commit to our relationships that are there to support us? Well, sometimes these people we really love just don't appeal to us – no fun anymore, not enough action, too boring. Actually, we can learn from these people. They are happy with whom they are and what they have become. They really piss me off; actually they are what I'm not. It's easy for them to just be still. Sometimes it's easy to manipulate the people who love us. So be careful; we don't want to hurt any more people today.

We should surround ourselves with healthy folks who will help with our accountability. Our accountability partners should not only call us on our stinkin' thinkin' but should, also, encourage us to go to our church and recovery meetings, etc., and should attend activities with us. We should encourage each other, share our hopes and desires for a real change in our hearts and be committed to doing what is right.

Saturday, I had the opportunity to talk with three young men from

Teen Challenge. One of the young men told me he was graduating in a few weeks. He said to me, "I've finally got it this time." What do you think of his statement? It scared me; I've said it too many times myself. My comment was, "Brother, be careful." Well, he left because he had it figured out and didn't want to hear anything I had to say.

Two of the men hung around to hear what I had to say. My point is I don't have the desire, but temptation is always there. I don't ever say I have it. I say I'm getting it every day. When I get to the gates of heaven, I'll know I finally got it. If I'm getting it, God will continue to help me witness, putting me in the right place at the right time.

When we are in the midst of sin, using or dry drunk or just exhibiting bad behavior, God doesn't call us, he's preparing us. I've said in the past, "I wasn't getting stupid, just making bad choices."

Commit means practice. We have to practice the principles in all our affairs. One counselor says commit means doing what you say you will do. Another counselor says commit means no matter what you have to sacrifice. We should sacrifice any of our own selfish needs and do whatever we promise we will do.

Psalm 31:4-5 reads, "Pull me from the trap my enemies set for me for I find protection in you alone. I commit/entrust my spirit into your hand. Rescue me, Lord, for you are a faithful God."

Psalm 37:5 says, "Commit everything you do to the Lord. Trust him, and he will help you."

Do you have any idea what God can do with you? You can reach a group of people to which the best or most renowned pastors could never witness or reach. So don't try to make excuses. God has picked you and knows you can do the job. Commit to God and know when he calls it's not about you but about Him. When God calls, listen. He's made the decision you are worthy of this job. We all have a need for more, bigger and better in our lives. Committing to helping others will bring us joy – the most awesome high you can ever have. While searching for more answers in our lives, our growth and connection with God and healthy Christian relationships make our recovery possible.

In Galatians 6:7-8, we read, "You will always reap what you sow! Those who live to satisfy their own sinful desires will harvest the consequences of decay and death. But those who live to please the spirit will harvest everlasting life from the spirit."

COMPASSION

It seems that every time something bad happens to us or to people in general, our first response is why me. How and why could this have happened?

Each of us has the gift of life that has been given back to us. We, in recovery, have a purpose to carry on the message. We have experiences, hopes and dreams to share with people who are struggling.

There comes a time when we need to share our pasts and offer advice. We need to be cognizant of when and how our help should be offered. When people are hurting, their lives are empty and their worlds have fallen apart, we need to offer them encouragement.

In an attempt to help, we offer all the inspirational and spiritual knowledge we have. There is nothing wrong with this as long as we don't come across as "preaching" to them. When someone is hurting and grieving, he needs sympathy and encouragement. We, better than anyone, know he needs our compassion.

It doesn't matter whose fault it is, if the pain is self-inflicted due to bad choices or due to uncontrollable circumstances. Now is not the time for confrontation. When his pain is the greatest, the fewer the words the better. The most comfort we can give is to put our arms around him and just love him. Love always wins. When we show compassion, we gain trust.

When the time comes that a person has endured all he can and is completely overwhelmed, he may ask for our help. We must be humble in our response. Now is the time for comfort and encouragement. Advice should be the truth as we know it, offered with the utmost kindness and sincerity.

None of us should try and go through tough times alone. We offer and do as much as we can for others. We confide and lean on each other. We must exhibit positive attitudes in our approaches to help. If a problem can not be rectified, let it go. Most problems will iron themselves out. Our best advice is not what we say but how we act and react.

The kindness that has been shown to us costs nothing to pass on to others. An encouraging word and an attitude of love and joy can make the difference in the life of someone who has given up hope. Just a smile can make a difference. We cannot keep what we have without giving it away.

How do we do this? We do this by trusting and believing in the love of Christ and by knowing his word is truth. Romans 8:28 says, "And we know all things work together for those who love God, to those who are called according to His purpose."

With our participation in recovery and our willingness to help others, we can fulfill His purpose for us. We then pray for guidance and direction in all situations and depend on it. God will give us the strength to carry on. Isaiah 26:5 says, "You will keep him in perfect peace, whose mind has stayed on you." Isaiah 30:15 says. "In quietness and confidence shall be your strength."

During my most desperate situations, my uncle Paul would send me the same words of encouragement - this too shall pass. We need to remind ourselves that hard times will pass with God's help. His promise says God is our refuge and strength, a very present help in trouble.

Remember we as Christians can edify God or destroy Christ in the name of Christianity. C. S. Lewis said the best argument for Christianity is Christians, their joy and completeness. He also said,

Christians are the strongest argument against Christianity when they are joyless, mean, narrow-minded and self-righteous. With this type of Christian, Christianity dies a thousand deaths.

One day there will be a judgment for each of us. All that will count will be the life we lived for God and the investments we made in the lives of others. When we get to heaven, we will take nothing. Matthew 7 says the road is narrow. We can leave behind a trail of encouragement and comfort that God is God, and God is love.

Through his compassion for me, I can recover from the troubles of the world. The proof of our Christianity comes not in what we say but in what we do.

COMPETITION

Webster defines competition as a contest between rivals. Competition is a part of our human nature, part of our makeup. God created it in all of us. We all have the desire to be the best, to be first, to impress someone. It is impressive to be a winner and come out ahead in everything we do. The downside is winning repeatedly can create arrogance.

Being arrogant doesn't show humility. Those with humility always think of their fellow man. Winning constantly and the drive to win at all costs create an attitude of deceit. It won't matter what it takes to win, but lying and cheating never honor a winner. It has always been my belief that if competition (winning) is our main focus in everything we do, we lose the ability to enjoy ourselves and the blessings that come with life.

The positive points in competition is it is exciting; it boosts morale and energy; it causes energy to flow. On the other hand it can occupy all the space in our minds, and we lose our focus on the task at hand. In competition there is the reality we can lose. Losing can take away our optimism and cause us to feel like failures. Instead of focusing on the negative points of losing, we should focus on the positive. Winning builds confidence; losing builds character.

Competition is a great motivator. It makes everyone work harder and allows us the potential to exceed expectations. We need to be cautious of how we use and allow our competitive nature to affect us. We should always allow God's character to shine in everything we do.

"Do you not know that in a race all runners run, but only one gets the prize? Run in such a way as to get the prize. Everyone who competes in the games goes into strict training. They do it to get a crown that will not last, but we do it to get a crown that will last forever" (1 Corinthians 9:24-25).

Our desire to win is to be a light to the world. Our purpose is to do our part in building the Kingdom. And win or lose, we will give the glory to God.

COMPLACENCY

Webster says complacence is the calm or secure satisfaction with oneself. Complacency is self-satisfaction accompanied with unawareness of actual dangers or deficiencies.

Complacency is a very dangerous place in which to be. It's a common attitude, especially after a brief amount of clean time and the first attempt at sobriety. Complacency says, "I've got this. I'm past that, over it. I'm more intelligent than addiction." It, also, says we're self-sufficient and need no help. We have developed too much confidence, and we even begin to get cocky.

Our self-centeredness expects everyone who supports us to go along with our decision to stop going to meetings and accept our logic for our lack of interest in staying in touch with our recovery programs. And we still have the audacity to expect praise.

By now, just our word that everything is under control is void. Our support usually can tell, even before we know, by our behavior that we need to call someone and stay connected.

The programs in Step 10 suggest that we continue to take personal inventory. If we get complacent, we put ourselves in jeopardy of relapse. We must ask continually, where am I right now, today? Recovering, not recovered!!!

I was asked once by my doctor and addictionologist, "Why won't you take your recovery seriously?" I thought I knew everything I needed to know and what I had was enough. Then my present therapist and accountability partner related his theory of complacency as being lazy. We're too lazy to seek the causes and answers as to how our behavior affects our thinking, our attitudes and our sobriety.

Laziness is a character flaw which refuses to recognize and commit to changing the behaviors that make our lives miserable and unmanageable. Boredom is created by laziness. If we are bored, we are not content; we want more than what we have. We are people who can not, do not and will not stay put. When we are disconnected from our support groups, addiction disguises the dangers of old acquaintances, places and things. These deceptions can cripple us. Changing the way we feel is a familiar addictive behavior. It takes a tremendous amount of energy, willingness and discipline to examine our behavior.

We cannot become complacent and quit on recovery. Consider the possibility we will always need to give our time and share our experiences with others. This keeps us focused and helps others. When it becomes inconvenient to show up and give back or we lose interest and find excuses to stay away, failure is possible and even likely.

Complacency, also, tends to have some relation to arrogance. We think we can do it our way on our own without help.

Continually removing ourselves from God shows we are too lazy and do not have the discipline to obtain the peace that is promised. Hebrews 6:11-12 says, "And we desire that each one of you shows the same diligence to the full assurance of hope until the end, that you do not become sluggish, but imitate those who through faith and patience inherit the promises."

CONFLICT

Nothing ever goes like I want it to! We as addicts have all sorts of conflicts in our plans and our jobs, with the laws and in most areas of our lives. Conflict in relationships is the most painful and normally causes the highest percentage of relapse. Long term success in recovery depends on a balance between our own personal tasks and our relationships. If we focus just on recovery and take our relationships for granted, our recovery will be at risk, and the people who support us will be hurt. If we continue to only care about ourselves, it will seem very familiar to them that nothing has changed.

When trying to reconcile relationships and restore trust, we first have to own up to our wrongs. Doing this may mean we have to swallow our pride and be humble. Don't make excuses. Don't use blame. Don't use guilt to manipulate or try to justify your wrong doings.

God teaches us to love even our enemies and to change our bad attitudes and behavior. It is even harder to do when these "enemies" are those closest to us. These may be the very ones we think hurt us. Sometimes tough love should hurt! God's love always allows us to forgive them, even if we are confused about where the fault lies. Always consider and have respect for the feelings of others. We can't argue their feelings.

In recovery we tend to get embarrassed that we have admitted we need help. Our old friends ridicule us to the point we can't take the pressure. Then we turn from the truth, our commitments, our support and ourselves. Many of our relationships from the past want us to fail; it makes them feel better about themselves. These people should be left alone.

Some of us thrive on disputes and arguments. Disputes lead to arguments. Normally, someone has something to gain or prove by being right. This type of behavior, when asking for help or reconciling a relationship, only makes the other person become defensive. At that point nothing can be called an accomplishment.

There are times when we should speak with our sponsor or accountability partner and/or get a mediator. Proverbs 15:22 reiterates this. Help from council can give us a different perspective. There we go again, asking for help one more time. Asking for help is new for us. Pride sometimes stands in our way of admitting we are wrong or asking for help. When we learn and practice God's advice, our pride lessens. After all, we are trying to reach a successful end or at least agree on a compromise.

Even in our best efforts, we have to expect and accept that every relationship we have wronged cannot and will not be worked out in a positive way. In working out what has been broken in any relationship, one person cannot be responsible for the outcome.

Romans 12:10 says, "If it is possible, as much as depends on you, live peaceably with all men." Remember any and all your relationships reflect YOU.

CONTENTMENT

There must be something in life besides the same old everyday nothing. It just seems there has to be more. I work hard, have some money, hobbies and collections, am involved in civic functions and the church, but it is not enough. I have lost interest and have nothing left in me. Nothing makes me happy.

One day something happened. I discovered the world of drugs; I thought I had found my solution. We all know the end to this story. My solution soon became my problem.

My problem began with me not being satisfied with myself. I was looking in all the wrong places to fill the void in my life.

When we can't find our niche and our purpose in life, we lose interest in even trying. We don't set goals. Our abilities are lost to our lack of ambition.

Why wasn't I contented? What exactly is contentment? Webster says contentment is to appease the desires of, to limit yourself in requirements, desires and actions. Contentment relates to having substance, to having meaning or significance, to being content, to quality of life.

To have contentment in our lives, we have to be passionate about something we hold dear to our hearts which in turn gives us purpose. Finding purpose gives direction, which allows us a sense of satisfaction when reaching goals.

While writing on this subject, I began to think about contentment in my own life.

I did a survey and asked others, "What is contentment to you?" Many of the answers were contingent upon finances. Before my journey through addiction, I dwelt on money, too. Now when someone asks me how am I doing, I often answer, "I am broker and happier than ever before and that doesn't make sense, does it?" It all has to do with being contented.

In getting to this place of contentment in my life, I had to become free from the bondage of many things. Of course, addiction was number one, but I, also, had to rid myself of pride, arrogance and selfishness.

Sometimes we have to be broken, stripped of external things, such as material wealth, to know if we are truly content or just happy because of what we have. The more we acquire, the more we want. We're never satisfied. This capitalist society in which we live teaches us to have a competitive spirit. We are always looking for a better job, more money, a bigger house or a finer car than our neighbors. Being content, I would realize I have enough and would actually cause me to share with my neighbors.

Then there is the productive minded or the workaholic who can't be still and enjoy life without thinking of something else that needs to be done. The workaholic is never satisfied until a job is completed, not content with just progress. But then completing a project only brings happiness until the next project arises. The workaholic is never content.

Is contentment a feeling or an attitude? A feeling is an emotional state, a responsive awareness or recognition of perception or thought or the capacity to respond emotionally. An attitude is a mental position in regard to a fact or state of mind or a feeling or emotion toward a fact or state of mind. I would say contentment is both a feeling and an attitude. Happiness is dependent on what is happening in the present, at this moment. Contentment is an inner peace and joy. You are "settled" in your heart, regardless of what is happening around you. You are not easily shaken when bad things happen.

Some say we shouldn't ever be content with just what we have; don't settle. As long as we are looking for contentment by society's standards, we will never have enough. There is always more to be had.

We hear of God as being a God of abundance, an abundance of grace and mercy. When we seek refuge in Him, we find peace and contentment. The apostle Paul said rich or poor, Christ is my Lord. Even those imprisoned can be like Paul. We may not be happy with the situation, but we have the joy of knowing Christ. We have the time to study God's word, to learn and reflect on choices and behavior. Our hearts can be content. Philippians 4:11 says, "Not that I speak from want, for I have learned to be content in whatever circumstances I am."

CONTROL

According to Webster's dictionary, control is to restrain, to regulate. A Bible concordance says control is order, rule or subdue. What can we control? The general consensus is nothing. We can't even control ourselves at times. While in active addiction, we try to control our lives and our use of drugs. Most of us were successful in the beginning. After we became productive in business, in charge at home and made decisions without failure, we basically thought we had it together. We had the idea we were in control because we always got our way.

At this point, our addiction has more authority, and we develop a sense of security and a bit of arrogance from our lack of failure. Some time may pass; our addiction begins to get stronger. We start making bad choices, and our ability to control situations starts slipping away. Our judgment becomes blurred, and we have no control over our mental state. We don't have the capacity to recover on our own.

We try desperately to regain self-control. Addiction teaches us survival skills. We sometimes use emotions, such as anger or the silent treatment, to control people by manipulation. Manipulation is a behavior that is important to recognize. Some of the time, it may work. Seemingly, for a short while people humor us by allowing us to get by with it. When we repeat ourselves over and over and try to control others, we set ourselves up for failure and more pain. We then find fault in their behavior in an attempt to make them feel guilty and to regain control.

After many times of failing to restrain from using or controlling how much or how little we used, we find ourselves out-of-control. We find we can't control much at all. We continue on to the bitter end – jail, institutionalization or death.

Are we uncontrollable people? What do you think? If we are in a confined area, we try to control what goes on in what we consider our space. Can we control our tongues? Can we control our hearts? Only when we give our hearts to God and practice diligently can we control our tongues. Psalm 19:14 says, "May the words of my mouth and the thoughts of my heart be pleasing to you, O Lord, my rock and my redeemer."

We can control the places we go. If by chance we can't, we can control what we do there. We can control our attitudes and the way we respond to people. Temptation will always show its nasty face. We can't control temptation, but we can control our response to it. God himself doesn't even try to control us. He gives us free will. He gives us the choice to resist temptation. 1 Corinthians 10:13 reminds us the temptations that come into our lives are no different from what others experience. God is faithful. He will keep the temptation from becoming so strong that we can't stand up against it. When we are tempted, He will show us a way out so we won't give into it.

We can't control the world, but we can control our salvation and destiny. God gives us the strength to control ourselves after all.

Repeat our Serenity Prayer. God, grant me the serenity to accept the people who can not change. Courage to change the One I can. And, wisdom to know it's Me.

COUNT IT AS LOST

In the very beginning of alcohol and drug use, we begin to lose. Intoxication causes memory loss. It may just be misplacing your keys or cell phone. At first, we just wonder what did I do. We then begin to lose some self-respect; a small amount of guilt and shame develops. Then we lose a bit of confidence that we can handle the drugs and alcohol, but most of us continue on the same path, hoping these are the only consequences.

As active addiction progresses, we begin to lose more, mostly monetarily in the beginning. Addiction had its way with us, and the money runs out. We start "losing" things valuable to us; we sell everything possible, even to family heirlooms, those things dear to our hearts that can never be replaced.

In our desperation, we make decisions that can and will affect us indefinitely. Each time a family member asks where something is, we are faced with our mistake, and the pain worsens. We are faced with truth or deception. Do I tell the embarrassing truth or do I lie?

Telling lies is one more example of how to lose relationships. People who care about us lose all confidence, trust and respect they once had for us. Our character diminishes as we use these people until they just simply have had enough.

There is something that happens, maybe in our subconscious. We've been "drugged" and have deceived others for so long that our deception no longer affects us. We no longer feel bad about it; we have lost the consciousness of what is right and wrong.

We, also, develop paranoia. Always in the back of our minds, we have the fear of getting caught, but at the same time our arrogance tells us we are too smart. Yet we do realize this has to come to some end.

Still we don't stop. We may lose everything – our jobs, homes and families. What do we have left to lose except our lives? Death may seem easier, the only way out. Don't judge those who choose this way out. But there is a way back for those of us who are willing to make the journey.

The secular recovery programs say drugs and alcohol only lead to jails, institutions and death. Many of us, the lucky ones, who find ourselves in an intervention instead of dead have options. We can go to rehab where we learn to put addiction into remission or we can end up in jail where we have no other alternative than to stop. In either situation we have a new chance at life.

In my experiences the secular programs offer a clean (without the use of drugs) way of life. Christ centered programs offer freedom from addiction through having a spiritual awakening and by developing a relationship with Christ Jesus. How does this happen? Scripture says in Matthew 16:25: "For whoever desires to save his life will lose it, but whoever loses his life for my sake will find it."

Since having a relationship with Christ, my old life has been put to rest. I can't forget it, but I can shut the door on it. With the help from new healthy relationships, my self-esteem can be rebuilt. With much hard work, some of those things I counted as being lost have been returned to me. In many ways I have more than I have ever hoped to have.

I have learned the true meaning of love. I now know the things that really bring me joy, and I no longer take relationships for granted. I can feel again!

I am blessed to have lived through the experiences of my past. I now live to share what God has done and continues to do in my life.

CRAVINGS

Behavior, whether it's good or bad, always begins with a thought. It's our nature to think about our own selfish desires first. We, also, deceive ourselves and think we are basically good and we are entitled to have a little fun. After all, no one will know.

We think we're strong; just one time will be safe. We begin to see all the grey areas instead of the black and white of right and wrong. Once we start riding the fence, we eventually have a weak moment. We then begin to rationalize our thoughts; they become a stronger temptation. We start focusing on our struggles at home and work; in our minds we think we need some relief. Then we think. "Well, I've done well for a while now. I deserve it." Society, also, teaches us to live for the moment.

Whatever sets us off, music, excitement, sexual gratification, our thoughts progress to a state of mental obsession. For us addicts having the chemistry that tells us we need a higher level of sensation, we are headed to self-destruction. When we obsess, the temptation gets stronger and stronger. We try to justify all the reasons why using is a good idea. By this time our behavior has begun to change, and someone in our network is asking questions. We say to ourselves, "He thinks I'm already doing it. I might as well." Giving in, we say, "I'm tired of fighting."

Most people think cravings come first. I have heard it said, "I had a dream and woke up craving." Cravings only come after we ingest the first drink or drug. The first one changes the way we feel and think. The Program says, "One is too many and a thousand is never enough."

After the first use, the drugs work only for a short time because of our guilt. All the old negative feelings begin once more, loneliness, dirty, worthlessness and shame. We have fallen off the wagon, let ourselves down and everyone else.

If we don't turn from our destructive thoughts before they become obsessions, we will lose. We lose strength, our health, momentum in our recovery and self-respect. We fall back into old miserable habits. Our choice of a solution for pain will never completely fill that hole. People, places and things can only pacify us for a short time. Our success can't fill it, the success of our spouse and children can't nor can our good works. God created this need only to be filled by God himself. Anything we do without God will be incomplete.

Frustrated and empty, we have a choice to make. We have temptation; we have a choice to or not to take that first drug. Temptation comes to us by Satan. Satan only has the power given to him by us. Addiction is "hell on earth." Satan doesn't hold the key to the gates; you and I do. We have the choice to reopen the gates, reclaim the misery and give up any progress toward recovery. The better choice would be to "hit your knees" when we have temptation.

Hebrews 2:18 says, "Since he himself has gone through suffering and temptation, he is able to help us when we are being tempted."

DARKNESS

In Isaiah 50:11 we read: "You who live in your own light will soon fall down in great torment." When our darkness is the greatest, we shouldn't focus so much on "why." We should ask God in prayer "what" he has for us to learn in this dark place. We too often try to change things on our own. It's not enough or fast enough for us at times; we want what we want now. We have to be still, quiet and wait.

Thank God we don't have to be afraid; his words tell us so. Psalm 112:4 says, "When darkness overtakes the godly, light will come bursting in. They are generous, compassionate, and righteous." Psalm 30:5 says, "Weeping may go on all night but joy comes in the morning."

When we listen and hear that voice inside, we come to realize we were never alone. In our worst moments, we learn our most valuable lessons. People will listen to our stories and our witnessing when it's obvious we have come out of darkness to the light. So walk tall and let the light shine in you!

"What I tell you in darkness, speak in the daylight from the house tops" (Matthew 10:27).

We read in Acts 26:18: "I am going to send you to open their eyes so they may turn from darkness to light, and from the power of Satan to God. Then they will receive forgiveness for their sins and be given a place among God's people, who are set apart by faith in me."

1 Corinthians 4:5 says, "Therefore judge nothing before the time, until the Lord comes, who will both bring to light the hidden things of darkness and reveal the counsels of the heart. Then each one's praise will come from God."

"He is the stone that makes people stumble, the rock that makes them fall. They stumble because they do not listen to God's word or obey it, and so they meet the fate that has been planned for them. But you are not like that, for you are a chosen people. You are a kingdom of priests, God's holy nation, his very own possession. This is to show others the goodness of God, for he called you out of the darkness into his wonderful light" (1 Peter 2:8-9).

DESPERATION

Everyone has some sort of desperation. I seemed to always be desperate to be accepted and find my place in life. I was eager to please people and had a hunger to fill an empty void on the inside. Even though I tried so hard to do good deeds and anything I could to gain popularity, there was something missing. There was a desire to change the way I felt.

I tried changing it in many different ways. I thought I had found it in drugs. The drugs worked for the short haul, but soon they began to cause more pain. Trying to change the way I felt became a hard and desperate way of life. I got married but still didn't feel quite complete. We got pregnant thinking a baby would fix us and fill that void. Instead I was now faced with the responsibility of supporting a family, a household and a habit. I thought with all the new pressure my drug of choice was not working, so I got desperate to find one that worked better. The new one worked for a short while, but just didn't do it for long.

I began to look around. It looked as if the majority of people who seemed happy possessed material wealth, big houses, fancy cars, etc. None of these things gave me comfort. Material wealth was not the answer. What did these happy people know that I didn't?

Maybe my choice was pain. I got desperate and ran from everyone and everything I loved. I just couldn't use enough to get away from myself. I was now desperate to get out of this mess. It seemed I couldn't be satisfied. My world began to crumble, and in a moment of clarity, I reached out for help.

With this human intervention, I found there were other people just like me. Our common denominator was the disease of addiction. I was told that I could be my problem. I didn't want to hear that. My thoughts were it couldn't be the drugs because they had worked before.

In desperation to avoid being caught, I ran from my new relationships, I lied to them and I stayed disconnected. I didn't want to be confronted so I at least slowed down for a while.

I have hurt so many relationships that now it's hard to find the courage to ask for help. I have tried everything I know to do. I just want some peace. I want to feel courage, desire, hunger and passion. I can not see for my desperation.

Desperation means the last resort. In John 21 we find when all else has failed, there was Jesus waiting by the fire. I have found comfort in Christ. Now in my new found freedom, I have the desire to be a follower of Christ and the passion for his character to be evident in me. He has given me the courage to go out and speak the truth about Him, to build his kingdom and to tell about the hunger that can only be satisfied by his word.

"Jesus replied I am the bread of life. No one who comes to me will ever be hungry again. Those who believe in me will never thirst" (John 6:35).

Matthew 5:6 says, "Blessed are those who hunger and thirst for righteousness, for they will be satisfied,"

It seems my desperation has changed. God has shown and given me a new purpose. My desperation is to fulfill this purpose and be pleasing to Him.

DON'T FORGET

Some of us, after being in recovery, forget we once were where many people are today. We tend to get the "holier than thou" syndrome. Can you remember when you were in such pain your life seemed to be over, when you became desperate and needed someone to be compassionate, someone to just say "things will be okay, this too shall pass." Can you think back to the time where the darkness overtook everything? You needed someone to say "I love you and together we'll get through this."

Many of us forget to show our concern when those in pain need someone to understand. Our own arrogance shows in a multitude of ways when we fail to show sympathy and concern. We might think "why can't they get it?" Or we might even think "I'm better than that." Have we forgotten where we once were?

When remembering where our lives once were, we should be charged with carrying on the message of recovery. The way to repay those who gave you a helping hand is to help someone else in need. You know their pain and suffering. Let them know they are not alone, that you care. Good will emerge from this.

There is a comradery among alcoholics and addicts; if you haven't lived it, you don't understand it. So who else is there better to help than us? Most of us are kind hearted and sensitive. We should be able to show compassion.

Most of us have issues with love. We have been hurt and let down so many times in the past we've often given up on love. In recovery we learn to love ourselves and our fellow man. Love is more than a feeling; it's choosing to behave in loving ways. The love of sharing recovery will teach and mature us as well.

Making a connection to someone in need can bring security to that person. He knows he is not alone - someone understands, someone cares.

Always keep in mind when you are offering your heart and help to someone that this could very well be an unrewarding undertaking. At first most people only want relief. We can offer all we have to give, but there has to be some self-protection. Galatians 6:1 says, "We should humbly and gently help someone onto the right path. And be careful not to fall into the same temptation." We can, also, invest too much time to their recovery and not enough to our own. Our own recovery is an ongoing process.

A believer who does not show love and compassion to a person in pain is not carrying out his responsibility as a Christian and is worse off than the unbeliever. God expects us to a witness. Admitting our own shortcomings will help others overcome their own shame and guilt.

In Joshua 10:26-27, Joshua wisely commanded his troops to not rest on their laurels or refuse to strive for continued victories but to complete the mission God had given them. For continued success in recovery, we can not afford to forget from where we came. We must carry on the message and help people who are hurting. In turn we are helping ourselves. Recovery is not for us alone!

EMPTY

In the beginning our curiosity about drugs showed us that "using" took care of not only our physical pain but also our mental and emotional pain. At first the drugs worked well. Then after some time, we began to develop a tolerance to the drugs and build up an immunity to them. That's when the drugs stop working. We neither get high nor do the drugs kill our pain. Yet we still continue to use more and more although they have no effect on us. We have managed to use, mis-use and abuse until we have crossed the line into dependency. Now using drugs is the only way we can function.

"Using" to function is a full time job. Addiction controls and manipulates our every thought; we're continually thinking how and where we can get the resources to get the drugs we need. Then we start using people, lying, cheating, stealing, whatever it takes at the time.

When we can't find what we need, the little pride we have left won't let us do some unmentionable things in order to get our drugs. There is a line most of us won't cross. What happens is we get depressed. Depression normally comes and goes because we find enough energy and resources to beat the system one more time. That's when we become careless and reckless; nothing matters. Morals and consequences never stop us.

There is a saying in the secular programs: Tired of being tired. One of the first questions I was asked after getting into a recovery program was "Are you tired of being tired?" Normally, when some type of intervention has begun, we are asked "What happened?" We usually are tired of chasing the insanity and are looking for a way out.

We usually have good intentions to stop the destructive behavior but not necessarily stop using. It's often been said, "I don't have another one in me." I say, "We do. It may be the last one, but we most likely do." When the air clears momentarily and we begin to feel human again, we find ourselves uncomfortable with our emotions and have the urge to change the way we feel.

As long as we have a small amount of pride, we will continue to try it again and again and will not ask for help. We at some point have to come to a place where we are tired of running, where our lives have become hopeless, and we are ready to give up. In reality the greatest place to be in active addiction is completely empty. Empty is where hurt, anger and fear no longer have any effect. The hurt becomes dull and has no intensity because we have no feelings. There is no fear when death seems like a relief. We can't get angry if we have no fight left in us. Empty, with no fight left in our being, recovery is then possible.

During my last twenty week stay in rehab, a friend wrote me a letter of encouragement. In the midst of catching up on the news at home and generally how everything was going and everyone was doing, he wrote, "Stop fighting. Jesus will fight the good fight for you." At that point I knew I had never completely surrendered to God.

Most of us know there has to be more to living life than the miserable existence we have experienced in the past. When we have fallen in a pit so deep that there is no one and nothing with us in this dark and empty place, then it is possible to slowly look up and see a glimmer of light. Maybe then all of us will realize the light we see can only come from God.

Many know that He is always faithful. We can make that 911 call to Him any time. Some of us use enough of God's word and scripture to avoid the issues which have strongholds on our lives. We can abuse grace. We will never recover by talking the talk. It is imperative we give up, allow ourselves to become empty and participate in God's program.

We read in Psalms 107:9-15:

> For He satisfies the thirsty and fills the hungry with good things.
> Some sat in darkness and deepest gloom, miserable prisoners in chains.
> They rebelled against the words of God, scorning the counsel of the most high.
> That is why He broke them with hard labor; they fell and no one helped them rise again.
> "Lord, help!" they cried in their trouble, and He saved them from their distress.
> He led them from the darkness and deepest gloom; he snapped their chains.
> Let them praise the Lord for his great love and for all his wonderful deeds to them.

EXPECTATIONS

When we have unfulfilled expectations, we get frustrated, feel let down or possibly think of ourselves as failures. In addiction when the drugs stop working, there are usually consequences, such as jail and institutions. At this point there is not much we can do except cope with it. There is something we can do about the bondage we allow to control us.

Our self-esteem has taken such a beating; we struggle with our expectations which only bring more pain with which to handle. We have not met our past expectations. Our past failures influence our expectations of future accomplishments and goals. Our perception of what we are capable of doing creates doubt. Then our standards are lowered; our goals are not set high enough to be challenging. Normally, we discredit our ability to succeed. Our behavior teaches us to set goals that are within our reach.

It has been said expectations of others is a premeditated resentment. If they don't do what I want, I'm gonna be pissed! Why do we expect people to accept us back into their lives with no expectations of us?

Now that we are in recovery, feeling physically fit and good about ourselves and even a little self-righteous at times, we tend to expect everyone else to be attentive to our every need. We may be the only one who thinks there has been a change. We normally don't get cooperation with our track record and continued selfish behavior. We have the audacity to expect something for nothing, expect it unconditionally with no questions asked. We really may be in a good place in recovery, but it's unfair to expect everyone to just accept it right away.

Patience is not one of our virtues. Recovery requires learning patience; anxious expectations, not getting what we want when we want it, can let us down, causing more pain. We can not control the feelings or actions of others. Furthermore, we shouldn't expect to be rewarded for our progress in recovery. We don't have the right to put the responsibility of our expectations on anyone.

We should look at another side of expectations. Are we selling ourselves short in our relationships with a spouse, significant other, family or friends? Do we put ourselves in a position to be demoralized and manipulated again into guilt and shame, making us feel we are not worthy of being treated fairly and loved without conditions. We do have options and can be loved unconditionally. We are worthy. God's word says, "All have fallen short of the glory of God." Don't belittle or beat yourselves up.

Sometimes it seems our families have expectations we can't meet right away. Instead of becoming frustrated, we should go to them humbly and explain that our old behavior was to try to please everyone, but today we must do one day at a time, one hurdle at a time.

Have we ever had expectations of God? Of course, we have. We, also, have been angry with God. We've all thought if there was a God, why is my life so miserable. Why doesn't He help me when I pray? Most of us have the misconception God punishes us for our wrongdoings. He gives us the rope to bind ourselves; it's called free will. God does not punish; remember He is a loving God. It is only He who unties the rope to set us free. He says He will walk through the fires in our lives and give us comfort in trials and suffering.

What does God expect of us in return? He commands us to love and obey. He says we are to give of ourselves and serve. Unselfishly for our comfort and peace, He offers us a relationship with him. He at times shows tough love, as in Hebrews 10:26: "When you know him and turn your back, He'll let you have this world without his blessings." However, whatever choices we make, God's expectations do not ever affect his acceptance and love for us.

Proverbs 10:28 says, "The hopes of the godly result in happiness, but the expectations of the wicked are all in vain."

FAILURE

Failure is a part of being human. In recovery we tend to identify ourselves as failures. Don't beat yourself up! There is no shame in failing. The shame is not admitting it and changing. Get up, dust yourself off and try again. Failure can teach us a much more valuable lesson than success if we become determined to succeed instead of giving up. Failure is an opportunity to learn and can promote growth.

Recovery is a learning process through failure at times. Failure can make us aware of our limitations and show us just how powerless we are without God and our new found relationships. Failure can destroy us or build us up.

We become depressed when all attempts are lost. We sometimes want to blame our failures on others when we have brought them on ourselves. Our selfishness is the most destructive behavior that makes us fail. Our pride won't let us step out and ask for help. Also, our pride tells us if we fail we are worthless. Most of us have a fear of failure even in recovery. We are so afraid of the unknown. Materialism fails us and leads us away from the importance of recovery.

Every area in our lives begins to fail while we are in active addiction. Our drugs fail us, our families and our friends. It seems that no one believes in us because of our past history.

When we do begin to recover, we have people in our lives who expect us to fail. We may have codependent family members who are not comfortable with change and will try to discourage us now that we have regained some control in our lives. After we have some control and are on a spiritual high or pink cloud, we feel as if we can handle recovery; we set ourselves up for failure. Before we fail at recovery, we have a choice to follow temptation or hand over our problems to God and ask Him, "What do I do and how do I do it?"

We then begin to see others fail. We become sensitive to their problems and are not so quick to judge. It's humbling to us all to help each other up.

The story is Jesus never feared failure of the things God told him to do and told him he could do. He had confidence in God; he had the responsibility to lead a group of people to recover from earthly behavior. How did he do it? He prayed a lot, he meditated and he stayed connected and in line with God's word.

We must stay connected to God. We, also, must stay connected to each other, pray for each other and pay our dues to recovery. We fail God a lot of times; It may seem He knocks us down, but He doesn't throw us away. He expects us to fail in order for us to be redeemed.

2 Corinthians 12:10 says, "Since I know it is all for Christ's good, I am quite content with my weaknesses and with insults, hardships, persecutions, and calamities. For when I am weak, them I am strong."

FEAR

I thought I had a plan. I knew what I wanted to do, but now I'm not so sure. All of a sudden I am afraid. Of what could I be afraid? Could it be the fear of the unknown? Yeah, that's it. There is always someone or something around the next corner with which we are not prepared to handle.

I have a fear of people, places and things. I have learned I have to be constantly aware of my surroundings. If I stay away from the wrong places, I won't see the people who most likely have the things I don't need. Well, then if I practice surrounding myself with good people, places and things, that's one small step towards getting through the fear of change.

It's common for most people to have a fear of failure. I think this fear directly affects us when we are trying new things. The fear of sobriety, being sober, goes right along with being afraid of failure. I'm so accustomed to using drugs to give me courage it just doesn't feel right without them. In the past drugs gave me energy and motivation.

Maybe fear can be a good thing. Knowing the drugs have started working against me, if I "use" I will probably become isolated, ashamed and depressed. My self-esteem will be shot not to mention the fear that my using will cause paranoia.

I, also, have a fear of rejection. We all fear rejection because we have been excluded before in our lives, such as in our relationships or job opportunities. We have a fear of not being accepted. We just haven't looked in the right places. Remember we don't get rejected because we are bad people; we get rejected because of our behavior.

It would be insane to do the same things expecting different outcomes. If we are rejected by someone or circumstances, we become rebellious, confrontational and angry. These actions only cause trouble and grief for us. It's all about our pride taking a hit. We act out; this keeps us from looking at ourselves.

My fear is someone will prove me wrong, call me on it. My pride tells me to do it my way and say "screw it" since everyone is against me. God give me the serenity to accept the things I cannot change, change the things I can.

Remember, I have recognized my arrogance. I can't do it alone, and I am worthy of God's love.

Do I fear God or do I fear hurting God? The Old Testament speaks of fear as being afraid of God. The Bible does speak of God's wrath for being disobedient. The New Testament speaks of fear as love or having respect for God. A healthy fear would be the fear of hurting God.

God's power starts with wisdom. We don't have to fear what people say or think.

Matthew 10:26-27 says, "Don't be afraid of people who threaten you. For the time will come when everything will be revealed; all that is secret will be revealed. What I tell you now in the darkness, shout abroad at daybreak. What I whisper in your ears shout from the housetops for all to hear!" When we tell our story openly and honestly, we don't have to fear being humiliated by others.

In Galatians 4:11, Paul wrote: "I fear for you. I am afraid that all my hard work for you was worth nothing." God wants to see the fruit of his labor; we should show our love and respect for his sacrifice..

Read chapter 4 of John. John 4:18 says, "Love has no fear because perfect love expels all fear."

We should remember as children of God, He loves us and gives us confidence. In Romans 6:15-16 we read: "You should not be like cowering, fearful slaves. You should behave instead like God's very own children – calling him Father. For his Holy Spirit speaks to us deep in our hearts and tells us that we are God's children."

Reading Romans 8:38-39, we find: "I am convinced that nothing can ever separate us from his love. Death can't, and life can't. The angels can't, and the demons can't. Our fears for today, our worries about tomorrow, and even the powers of hell can't keep God's love away."

Luke 2:10 says, "The angel reassured them; Don't be afraid! I bring you good news and great joy for everyone."

FED UP

What is it going to take? Enough is enough! Sick and tired of being sick and tired? Fed up?

Are you fed up with the way things are, tired of this life the way it is, tired of the never ending misery? Are you tired of being controlled by the drugs, sick of the dysfunction? Fed up with your bad choices? This is insane. Are you fed up with the guilt and shame, going places and ashamed to hold your head up?

At times it seems we don't have a choice except to continue on this destructive path. There is another choice! But we have to get to a place where we are fed up enough that we are willing to fight for recovery and not settle for just doing better. In the beginning of recovery, sometimes we have to hang tough, taking baby steps until it gets easier. Be careful! When things begin to get better, we tend to let our guard down. This is the time to buckle down and say, "I will not give up on recovery." We can't afford to be satisfied or comfortable in recovery.

Change is uncomfortable for the most part, but it's worth it to work through the pain and find joy. It's often said, "Anything worth having is worth fighting for." It's very painful and it takes a lot, no, an incredible, amount of energy to face the pain that caused our problem and the problems and consequences our addiction created.

We have to get fed up and face reality. We are spoiled people by nature and want to be completely satisfied at all times. We have to go through discomfort to be successful in recovery. It will only last for a season.

One of the most common thoughts or ideas about recovery is using has become miserable and we want relief that recovery can bring. Recovery is not easy and is not comfortable most of the time. Our nature or addictive behavior says I know how to stop this uncomfortable feeling. Even when we're not using, people may be suspicious of us. This is frustrating and seems like a good excuse to say if they think I am, I might as well. It's not; this would be the worst time of all to give up now.

We understand it is not all that easy to just make up our minds to stop; others don't. Our families and loved ones get fed up long before we do. This doesn't mean they stop loving us; they just get sick and tired and worn out with our excuses, deceit and manipulation. They have earned the right to mistrust everything we say and do.

We are all taught God loves us unconditionally; that's the Gospel. But God gets fed up, too! He gets fed up with our 911 prayers and our broken promises. He gets fed up with our bad choices and shows us tough love. When we turn our backs, He allows us to do it our way.

God can and will deliver us in an instant, but from that point we have to participate in his program. Jesus paid the price for our sins and gave us freedom from bondage. When we get caught up in worldly behavior, we put ourselves back in our prison. "If we willfully sin after knowing the full knowledge of the truth, there is no sacrifice for sin, but a certain judgment and a fiery indignation, which will devour his adversaries" (Hebrews 10:26-27).

FEELINGS

Everyone has feelings. No one likes uncomfortable feelings, much less those deeply painful ones. Some people, in an attempt to avoid or diminish these feelings, isolate the feelings and put them out of their minds. After all, if you don't acknowledge something, it will go away! That may work sometimes but not if you're passionate about those particular feelings.

For the other people, us with addictive disorders, using drugs has become the way to stop the pain we are feeling. After our use has progressed to dependency, we magnify our pain by drug induced negative feelings which include fear, distress, desperation, helplessness, hopelessness and the list goes on and on. Anger is, also, an uncomfortable feeling.

Life, itself, gets to the place where it's the primary reason we need to change the way we feel. If we feel anything it's probably the guilt and shame for our actions, the way we hurt people. It hurts us to feel!

Then we find our lives have become unmanageable. Most of us are still so full of pride and arrogance we say we don't need help, we can handle it on our own. Now the feeling of desperation overwhelms us. We are either desperate to get more drugs or desperate enough to ask for help. Desperation wins out over pride. We steal, fight, run or ask for mercy. Unfortunately, some of us die.

Early in recovery we tend to go through more pain; we begin to feel the pain we have caused for ourselves. We sometimes feel lonely and depressed and easily become over sensitive and get emotional. We are so far removed from love and compassion for people, it hurts. Addiction has taken away any joyful feeling we had.

Feelings are very deep and complicated. People can't agree or disagree with us. Most everyone, addict or not, think first of their own feelings. Feelings can get us in trouble in recovery. Our feelings may tell us we are in a good relationship. The majority of the time we make decisions based on a thought. In most circumstances we should listen to our hearts.

In recovery we learn how confused we really are. We are taught to give every thought a thorough examination; is this relationship a good or bad choice? Our minds say one thing, our hearts says another. Sometimes we feel it's the only choice we have. Being emotionally involved, we're too close. We may be feeling a sense of attachment. We may make a choice out of desperation in an attempt to fill a void or to avoid rejection.

Recovery has begun when we start noticing the small things, when we are comfortable with just being still to the point we can feel a peaceful quiet silence without distraction. It feels good to look in the mirror and feel okay with the person in the reflection. Everyday things happen; our feelings continually change from good, bad, right or wrong.

Occasionally we find it hard to feel God's presence; we feel far removed from his mercy. We feel unworthy of his love and our hearts feel empty. Joshua 1:5 says, "I will be with you; I will not fail you or forsake you." When we struggle with our feelings and try to reconcile them, we should study and see if either our minds or our hearts line up with God's word.

FORGIVENESS

We focus on the pain others have caused us; we may focus too much and use it as an excuse for our behavior. Many times our hurts are valid, but sometimes what we think was unacceptable, unthinkable and inexcusable was only our perception of what happened, clouded by our sensitivity. Until we start to make sense of our pain and see the greater good in our trials and tribulations, we feel like the victim. Often times we are an easy target since we already feel guilty about our personal failures.

Now God is aware of what we are going through. He has a plan where our struggles will change our lives for the better. Be encouraged; we gain through our pain.

I ask the question, "Is it hard to be a God follower?" Then I remember a very important topic in my recovery – forgiveness. I have to understand I am supposed to forgive others as God forgives me.

To forgive is to give grace. Grace is unmerited favor, something we don't deserve. We can forgive without letting the offense consume us. Forgiveness is not pretending something didn't happen. We should address the issue directly, not avoid it. If necessary, we may need to avoid the other person involved.

Forgiving is not excusing or forgetting. It means this part of the story is over. Otherwise, we'll keep dragging up the painful past. We have to acknowledge when something needs to be over. Forgive, and when we've done all we can do, we should dust ourselves off and move forward.

Forgiving is not foolishness. It's choosing to see that person differently. Take into consideration we may not even be the problem. That person may be just unloading their frustration on us. Maybe we're the last straw that broke the camel's back. By the same token, we have to honestly acknowledge our part in the situation.

Forgiving is neither excusing it nor giving the okay to do it again. We just need to reroute our thoughts and give them to God and let him deal with them. We give forgiveness because it's given to us as easily as asking for it.

We don't have the right to not forgive ourselves. God doesn't put qualifications on forgiveness; He doesn't say I'll forgive you "if." We shouldn't put standards on our faults and failures. God wants us just as we are. We can be victorious and overcome our struggles by not giving up, by believing God will bring us through.

Being forgiven for our actions does not excuse them or make them right. When we forgive, it doesn't mean we excuse. We identify with how we have been hurt and turn the problem over to God. This helps us let go of the pain and keeps us from using it to continue our bad behavior.

"If you forgive those who sin against you, your Heavenly Father will forgive you. But if you refuse to forgive others, your Father will not forgive you" (Matthew 6:14-15).

FREEDOM

How do we become free? How do we keep this freedom? At first there is a real bondage, a stronghold on our lives. We begin to wonder what happened. The very thing that seemed so wonderful, the thing that made problems go away doesn't work any longer. Just like other love affairs that fizzled and stopped giving us that warm tingling feeling, this one, too, seems to have run its course. We need to call it quits.

We should stop now, but we keep thinking this time will be different. The real truth is it never is as good as it was the first time. The drugs just don't work anymore. The problems, the consequences, the hurt or broken relationships, our self-esteem, our appearance and the way people treat us can't be fixed by drugs. Drugs didn't cause our problems, but they certainly made them worse. A cause can't be a cure!

We have to do something different this time. In my life I've noticed the people I consider godly seem to be happy. They must really be Christians. What can I do to be like them? They can just sit, be still, be quiet or talk and enjoy the simple things in life.

If all else fails, try God. I'll ask God to help me with this new lifestyle. I've heard "let go and let God." I did all these bad things so I'll be honest and admit them. I'll forgive anyone I have anything against and I'll ask forgiveness from those I hurt. I'll walk like a Christian with integrity, have good character and be a trusted servant to help others. I'll get busy and find a church to glorify God; I'll let God teach me.

I'll get involved in Bible studies, service work, helping others, NA, AA and other activities that keep me busy living right.

I'll want to share my experiences and hopes with others in trouble. John 14: 26-27 says,

When the Father sends the counselor as my representative, and by counselor I mean the Holy Spirit, he will teach you everything and will remind you of everything I myself have told. I am leaving you with a gift – peace of mind and heart. And the peace I give isn't like the peace the world gives. So don't be afraid or troubled.

In Jeremiah 1:6-9 we read: "I can't speak for you. I'm too young. The Lord said don't say that. Go where I send you. Don't be afraid. I will be with you and take care of you. The Lord touched my mouth and said see I have put words in your mouth." We can only keep what we give away.

Remember we are clean and have a conscious, constant contact with God. We are sober. Ask to be released from our general curses and learned behavior. I didn't say to be released from our disease, but our life is a life of dis-ease without God. He can and will give us freedom.

It's not hard to be free. God only wants our devotion and obedience. Pray everyday; commit to prayer. Share your new found freedom. "I will sing about your flower. I will shout with joy each morning because of your unfailing love. For you have been my refuge, a place of safety in the day of distress" (Psalm 59:16).

FRIENDS

How do we measure the value of our friends? During active addiction, we establish a relationship with our dealers. After all, they're the ones with the drugs. When we have the need to fill an emptiness, they're there with the answer. When we're wracked with pain, they're there with drugs to kill the pain. Because they provide relief for us, we think we've found our new best friend. Feeling "high" makes us feel close to the supplier.

Many times the dealer will give us the impression of caring about us, especially if we spend a lot of money and do not become a financial or dependent burden on their profit. In reality, they care nothing about our well being. And at some point in our addiction, we become unstable and thus are actually a risk to them.

The truth is we can't form good, healthy, stable relationships during active addiction. We're lucky if some of our real friends stick with us through our addiction.

When addiction progresses to the point we become isolated, we think no one cares; we feel alone without a friend in the world. Most of us want to blame everyone and everything rather than recognize and accept that we're the problem. It was we who pulled away, not our dear friends who never gave up on us. Sometimes we pulled away because we were ashamed and didn't want to expose our friends to our world of addiction.

Even in recovery our addictive behavior has us measure friends by how much or how little they do for us. We value them by the actual amount they spend on us. We even have the audacity to feel hurt when they cut us off. We act as if they are the enemy when we can no longer manipulate them. We get angry and pull away. When we can't use people anymore, we just cast them aside.

We need to hook back up with our true friends when we are healthy enough. They will love and support us just as we are.

So, what is a friend? A friend is a favored companion, valued with high regard, attached to one another by affection, serving a beneficial purpose, comforting to one another by mutual association and actions.

A friend gives of himself without expecting anything in return. A friend never abuses the other's kindness. A friend loves so deeply that he feels your hurt and pain. To have a friend requires being a friend. If you want others to support you, support them. When you need help yourself, offer to help a friend. You'll be surprised what you get in return. If you need to be loved, show love. Love your friends unconditionally, and they will love you. If not, they weren't true friends from the start.

"I command you to love each other as I have loved you. And here is how to measure it – the greatest love shown here is when people lay down their lives for their friends. Now you are my friends. You didn't choose me, I chose you, so go and produce fruit" (John 15:12,13,15,16).

None of us has ever experienced having a friend like the friend we have in Jesus. Jesus shares with us everything his father taught him. Jesus will befriend us in good and bad times. He teaches us to be accountable, responsible and trustworthy. Jesus teaches us how to be a friend to others.

FRUSTRATION AND ANGER

Anger is simply an emotion that comes from being irritated. Depending on how offended we are, anger can turn into hostility and rage. When we don't let anger go, it becomes resentment. We hold a grudge and allow ourselves to get frustrated and angry over and over again.

We repeat this behavior. We call it losing our temper, being ticked off, being POed. This is the negative side of anger. There can be a positive side. It's been said anger releases energy into our nervous system. It's our choice to use this energy in a constructive or an abusive way.

When anger controls us, it's unhealthy. We always think of revenge first, what we can do to retaliate. We aren't thinking clearly or rationally. At this point our emotional, physical and verbal actions become destructive. Our anger can even keep our minds so defensive it blocks our ability to love.

Most of us with anger problems walk around with it on the surface. Anger is evident in our appearance and actions. We're ready for confrontation. Others seem to have a calm demeanor but are ready to explode from bottled up anger.

We like to blame others for our anger. Wrong! People don't "lose" their temper; they "choose" their temper. Consider our anger as a reaction in which we "use" because of pain, hurt or fear. Anger is secondary to these emotions.

I realize my anger seems to overcome my fear. Being sensitive, I'll get hurt just so many times before I respond in anger. We have been hurt or afraid of someone or something so often that anger has become a defense mechanism for us. Frustration is not as offensive; it's usually born out of unfilled expectations, expectations of ourselves or others. Most times if we'll take an honest look at the big picture, we'll recognize this particular problem just isn't that important after all. No one likes to be controlled by anger.

When our hearts are controlled by the Holy Spirit, our anger can be healthy. The most constructive ways to deal with anger is to speak openly and honestly with a loving attitude. We should make amends quickly if we have wrongly spoken in anger. We'll regret it later if we don't. Also, we should not pretend to never get angry. This only turns our feelings into resentment. We must settle our differences with others or Satan wins.

"Be angry, and do not sin. Do not let the sun go down on your wrath. Nor give place to the devil" (Ephesians 4:26-27). Let the Holy Spirit control you and deal with anger constructively.

GIVING UP

I have recently been involved in helping a friend, yet again, get into rehab. Sammy and I met at a wonderful Christian program in North Georgia, Victory Home. We lived together, shared experiences and became friends. He and I learned we were alike in many ways. We were both addicts with self-esteem problems. The two of us were spoiled by our parents' success. We both did our jobs as addicts very well, such as manipulating our families to get what we wanted and lying to cover our tracks.

Normally, neither Sammy nor I would have done the things we did, but addiction made us do things we never thought we'd do. We developed bad behavior in order to survive; then came the guilt and shame. After many failed rehabs and countless attempts at sobriety on our own, we progressed deeper into the grips of addiction.

There are several types of rehabilitation programs available to addicts like us. Secular programs teach spirituality but are confusing at times. These programs speak of a higher power but are not allowed to call the power by name because this might offend someone. The secular programs teach that our disease progresses. Each time we relapse, we get worse. We get worse physically, mentally, and emotionally.

Our last resort was to try God, a Christian program; nothing else had worked. God's word in Hebrews 10:26 says, "When we have the knowledge and know the truth about Christ and turn our backs, there is no sacrifice for sin. He will throw you back into the consuming fire."

God will throw us back into the real world letting us do things our way. This shows God's tough love. Relapse will progress rapidly.

Some of us get the idea about recovery and avoid extended suffering. Others, like Sammy and me, are prideful and arrogant. Pride says we're better than that and too good to live under certain conditions. Arrogance says we're more intelligent and can beat the system on our own.

In desperation, when our way stops working, we make a 911 call to God. We promise to never do this again if God will only help us out of this mess. God has faith in us and will love us no matter what. Then we feel better physically and mentally and have the idea we've had enough recovery. We say, "Okay, God, I've got this!" We have only convinced ourselves we are in good shape, in a good place. We then have the tendency to become complacent and get careless. At this point it is inevitable we will fail at recovery once more.

Another bond Sammy and I share is misery. A couple of years ago, I was so miserable I gave up. I was too tired to fight. I surrendered everything I could to God. He taught me how to let go of myself completely and trust him. I am not saying I am all I want to be. I'm saying I thank God I am not who I once was.

At first in 1 Timothy 6:11 God said, "Run from all these evil things and follow what is right and good. Pursue a godly life, along with faith, perseverance, and gentleness." Then He taught me I had to be beaten down and broken before He could make me new. He then gave me the courage to go to war with him. Verse 12 says, "Fight the good fight for what we believe."

God's promise to Peter while waiting by the fire in John 21 says, "I'll go through the fires with you if you walk with me." We can not fight our battles alone. The last book in the Bible, Revelations says God wins!

I called to check on my friend last week. His mom said to me, "Sammy is giving up." I said to her that is what God has been waiting to hear. Sammy is studying and has enrolled in God's program, the only perfect recovery in existence.

I will never give up on recovery; it's not in me to quit. My prayer for you today is that you experience the whole "peace" and freedom God offers and not just the small "piece" of recovery we find here and there.

In Exodus 14:13-14, Moses told the people to not be afraid, to stand where they were and watch the Lord rescue them. The Lord would fight for them. They wouldn't have to lift a finger in their defense.

GOALS

Most of the battles in life are fought within our inner-selves. What makes our problem more significant is that it's ours and our battles with addiction own us. It's human nature to think of ourselves first. This doesn't mean we don't care about other people and their problems or we don't have kind and sensitive hearts. It's just that we have become selfish and self-centered. We have to get right with ourselves before we can get right with others. To get right, we must set and meet goals.

The first goal should be to find the right tools that work for each person individually. These may be counseling, meetings, support groups, church, Bible study or all of these. Be careful to not overload or have your plate too full. We want our plans and goals to be achievable. If not, we will feel as if we've failed and cannot even get recovery right.

Goal two should be to commit to your program and be open to suggestions. A closed mind and bad attitude will rob you of important necessary details. We have to recognize our arrogance and admit to not knowing everything about recovery. When we learn that this process of addiction and recovery is no game and become willing to apply ourselves, we begin experiencing some good results. Trials will always come our way. Staying connected and having a strategy help us follow the rules. Doing this, we know what to do when temptation or danger comes our way. Wandering around lost, alone and reclusive almost always guarantees failure.

The third goal is to get real, be honest and develop new habits.

Tell the truth always. It may sting and be uncomfortable at first, but it gets easier. We will be wrong and make mistakes many times. Just be truthful about them. See this as growth and move on. We will gain maturity from these experiences. We will eventually regain trust and respect from our relationships. The truth will also allow loved ones to recover; they deserve recovery, too.

Get real! We cheat ourselves by avoiding the hardest and darkest places and truths about recovery. This can undermine or lessen our potential to succeed. Early in recovery most of us are not strong enough to try and tough it out. In thinking we can, we only deceive ourselves and others. It's only our pride disguising the fact we still have addictive behavior and really need help. When we choose to tough it out alone, the potential for unwanted consequences and suffering increases, and relapse is inevitable.

After getting real, making plans and setting goals in recovery, we are then faced with balancing our time between goals, family, friends, jobs, hobbies and time alone with God. It is of the utmost importance to remember – one goal at a time, one day at a time!

"I am still not all I should be, but I am focusing all my energies on one thing, forgetting the past and looking forward to what lies ahead. I strain to reach the end of the race (the goal) and receive the prize for which God, through Jesus Christ, is calling us up to heaven" (Philippians 3:13-14).

GRATITUDE

According to the Bible gratitude is thankfulness. Webster defines gratitude as an emotion of the heart. Feeling grateful is a pleasing, satisfying feeling.

As people suffering from a dependency, we have become accustomed to instant gratification, living life in the fast lane. Our minds have become programmed by our drug use; we have the need to change the way we feel. Most people can enjoy normal tasks and participate in activities with a normal kind of patience. We, on the other hand, get impatient and stressed easily; we begin to take short cuts that look and feel much like a quick fix. The quick fix is not gratifying or satisfying and is never enough.

Recovery, at times, is painful, too slow, unpleasant and unpleasing. We may think our thoughts are good, but our decisions may cause a chain reaction of bad events. We get uncomfortable; then we relapse.

I am grateful to be able to recognize when a situation can be risky, recognize the good and bad choices and then choose the good. I am a grateful recovering addict!

I am grateful for getting caught! I've heard statistically 88% of us at least slow down when we are about to be caught. 65% have a fear of someone finding out their secret, finding out they're not the person everyone thought they were. 97% are afraid of getting caught and the consequences thereafter.

There are some rewards for getting caught. The secret is out in the open. Thank God, it can finally be over. There will be no more deception. I hate lying, cheating, stealing, etc. I can now be open and honest. I am grateful people still love me and want to help me. I am grateful to be forgiven by those I have hurt. I am grateful for good healthy relationships. I am grateful for a program that helps me recover and helps me carry my load. I'm grateful for living one step at a time, one day at a time.

Most of all I'm grateful for God who forgives me and gives me abilities and talents and allows me to do things I could never do on my own. I am grateful to be one of God's children, to be accepted and loved just as I am, to be secure and protected and to be significant in his eyes. God gives me a purpose.

GUILT AND SHAME

Guilt is an emotion recognized by our consciences, hearts and minds. Addiction creates and multiples our guilt and shame. There is a difference in "being" guilty and "feeling" guilty. If we actually, physically or mentally, commit an offense which is morally wrong, we are guilty. If we fall short of another person's expectations, we feel guilty. This does not necessarily mean we should. It just means that emotionally we are sensitive people who don't like to let others down.

We can be guilty of hurting people and not even realize it, because we have repeated the offense so often we've become desensitized to our bad behavior. Most of us have always had a sense of God's presence but try and push him into the background when we're doing wrong. Our drugs kill the pain and repeatedly hide our emotions and dull our consciences. Therefore, as our drug use progresses, our guilt and shame are lessened.

In recovery when we become clean and sober, we begin to get in touch with our emotions and can feel again. At this point we have to distinguish between the guilt that is earned and that which is unnecessary.

We know when we've offended someone, it's our responsibility to make things right. If our guilt is too much to handle, it gets in the way of recovery. We feel the need to ask for forgiveness but should try to make amends only if it doesn't hurt us or others. If we're not sure, we should talk with our sponsors or accountability partners. Asking forgiveness or saying "I'm sorry" loses its effectiveness if we keep repeating the same offense again and again. In most cases forgiveness does not come from what we say but from what we do, our actions.

When we know we have not intentionally offended someone, we acknowledge it and confront the situation in a nonconfrontational manner. One way is to say, "I've done the best I could with the resources available to me. I won't let you put me on a guilt trip today." We are human and shouldn't punish ourselves for human error. When it's an honest mistake, correct it and move on.

Recovery has begun when we can identify and understand our emotions and let go of our past guilt and shame. Christ didn't come to condemn us and make us feel guilty and ashamed. Christ came to cleanse our sins and make us whole again.

"For all have sinned and fallen short of the glory of God" (Romans 3:23). "According to my earnest expectations and my hope, that in nothing I shall be ashamed, but that with all boldness, as always, so now also Christ shall be magnified in my body, whether it be by life or death" (Philippians 1:20).

HABITS

Webster defines habit as a manner in which we do things naturally or aptitude acquired by practice. Where, when and how did habits become second nature? If we examine our lives, we know we developed our habits by seeing, hearing, watching and imitating those who influenced and shaped us - our leaders, parents and peers. It is evident habits are learned from the people in which we surround ourselves.

We live in a social world; almost everything we do requires interaction with others. These people make impressions and influence our lives in one way or another. When we have good influences and make good choices, our outcomes are more apt to become positive. We repeat those choices, and good habits begin to form.

What about those poor influences and bad choices? When our outcomes are bad but seem to be successful for others, we tend to repeat the actions again until we develop the habit. At some point as addicted people, we have to realize it's not working for us. These bad habits we have developed are the only way we know to live. Sometimes the hardest part of learning how to change our habits is to unlearn the old way of doing things.

Then there is the fact that using alcohol or drugs is our excuse to justify having made bad choices. Or do we deny that drugs had anything to do with our behavior? 85 to 90% of alcoholics/addicts are quite sensitive people. I prefer to think these people are good at heart and would not do most of the things we do if they weren't addicted.

How do we change our bad habits? We change by gaining knowledge and understanding, by falling down and getting back up, by never giving up. Knowledge is a powerful tool. The more knowledge we have, the more simplistic our behavior seems and the more confidence and control we have to make good decisions. It is apparent being stable emotionally makes it easier to recognize how much any given situation can affect us in our relationships, careers and recovery.

If we are under the influence, we are emotionally unstable, so circumstances control us. When continually making and living with destructive habits, our quality of life is just existing from day to day. As we gain in knowledge and become stronger, we then start managing our lives and functioning as human beings. It is evident we must learn new things to make better choices and develop new habits.

With clear minds and using new healthy attitudes, skills, abilities and behavior, we can experience the rewards of good choices and develop healthy habits. We now have the option to change or cling to our old destructive ways. "If it is disagreeable in your sight to serve the Lord, choose for yourselves today whom you will serve: whether the gods which your fathers served which were beyond the river or the gods of the Amorites in whose land you are living; but for me and my house, we will serve the Lord" (Joshua 24:15).

Joshua 22:5 says, "Make it a habit to obey all the commands Moses gave you. Love the Lord your God, walk in all his ways, obey his commands, be faithful to him, and serve him with all your heart and all your soul."

HONESTY/LYING

Do I have the capacity to tell the truth? Jeremiah 5:2 says, "Even when under oath, as surely as the Lord lives, they all tell lies."

Even when caught, I would lie. My wife would look at me and ask, "What's wrong with you?" I'd say, "Nothing. What's wrong with you?" I'd turn the question around on her so she's think maybe she was wrong.

My brother approached me about slowing down. I told him I wasn't doing anything wrong. He told me he knew I was lying but, also, knew I didn't want to lie to him.

How honest do we get? Someone tells something about me or confronts me and gets one little part wrong. Well, that's enough for me to turn the situation around to suit myself. I still have a problem with someone else telling my story. It's mine; let me tell it. Do I want to leave out parts? Do I tell it to suit the listeners? Am I just not ready to be honest?

Lying has become a way of life! My dad once told me if you tell one lie you have to tell another to cover up the first one. How do we stop this cycle? How do we get completely honest? Truth, accountability, integrity and character will get us there.

Honesty gets easier as we practice. Get an accountability partner you trust. Tell him everything; share the good and the bad. Telling the truth gets easier, becomes more natural. When we become involved with healthy people, we tell the truth.

When we say we'll do something, we do it. This shows integrity. It always makes me feel good to receive praise after doing what I've promised. Even if I'm not praised, I can hold up my head and say I did what I was supposed to do.

I have promised God I would witness for him, tell people about him. I am now accountable to God. Ecclesiastes 4:9 tells us, "Two get a better return for their labor." Verse 12 further tells us, "A cord of three is not easily broken." God is in the midst of any relationship.

There are times our accountability partner won't be available. People will let us down. At these times, just remember God is always available and will never let us down. We all need that cord of three!

HOPE

The Bible says hope is an expectation or expect with confidence. Webster defines hope as a desire of some good, accompanied with a belief that it can be obtained; trust; someone or something on which trust and confidence are placed.

Faith and hope go hand in hand. Faith is believing without seeing, feeling without being touched, knowing we are never alone. Hope is actually being able to see ourselves in our future, where we want to be. Hope is essential to having a positive attitude and good health. Hope opposes depression. Healthy emotions have hope. Unhealthy emotions have the potential to become depressed.

We have to will ourselves to have hope even when our destination seems too far away to reach. In the past, we wished for things in our lives, promises were broken, our expectations fell through and our hope began to dwindle away until there was no hope left. We lose faith; depression takes over.

We are talking about placing our hope and trust in people. We sometimes place our hope and trust in the wrong people, or we rely too heavily on our therapist, the program, our sponsor, our husband or wife or another addict who's still struggling to stay clean. We place our recovery in their hands. Depending on other people to give us our freedom is a bad choice.

We find ourselves struggling, barely holding on, losing more and more hope. We get angry, hurt or ashamed because we feel we've let someone down. We get frustrated and give up.

This is when we should turn to God. He gives us everlasting hope. No matter how terrible the battles we face, if and when we turn to the Lord, we will have hope. "Cursed are those who put their faith in mere humans and turn their hearts away from the Lord" (Jeremiah 17: 5). Verse 7 says, "Blessed is the man that trusts in the Lord and whose hope the Lord is."

HURTFUL WORDS

Words used and expressed in the wrong manner can be hurtful and dangerous. Often times we don't think before we speak. When angry or disappointed, we let our feelings get involved when we shouldn't.

Take the word disappoint. You have disappointed me. We've all heard this at some point in our lives. People with low self-esteem are especially sensitive to this. They often misconceive and misconstrue what is said. Sensitive people take everything to heart.

Using the word disappoint separates one from another. Someone can spend the rest of his life trying to please or mend the gap made by the disappointed person.

When someone has done wrong, call him out on it, but be aware of your terminology. Confront the offense but don't attack the person. Approach the person and correct the offense. The correction should not sound personal. We should take our own agendas out of the situation.

My wife always says, "It's not about who is right or wrong, it's about what is right or wrong." Confront the problem, not the person. Taking back words is like trying to put toothpaste back in a tube; it can't be done.

Exodus 4:12 says, "Now then go, and I, even I, will be your mouth and teach you what to say."

In Jeremiah 1:9, scripture says, "Then the Lord stretched out His hand and touched my mouth, and the Lord said unto me, Behold I have put words into your mouth."

Let us all remember this scripture from James 1:19-20: "Everyone must be quick to listen, slow to speak and slow to anger. Exercising God's words help us to choose our words, choose our tempers and not lose our tempers."

My prayer: God don't let me hurt anyone today with the words that come from my mouth.

I

~~~ⅿⱺⱺⱸⱺⱺⱸⱺⱺⱮⱮ~~~

This is a story between a recovering addict and a codependent wife. It's filled with good intentions, poor decisions, misunderstandings and God's intervention.

My partner and I have a prison ministry that, in a way, has become my new addiction. Actually, I love this ministry so much I sometimes put it before my family and my work. It is so rewarding to me; I think about it seven days a week. What I'm saying is I think it has been and is the best thing for my recovery.

What's wrong with this picture? I, I, I!

So this story begins with Steve and I having some ladies in class tell us there were others who had shown an interest in our classes but couldn't attend because their jobs were at night. He and I discussed maybe having Saturday night classes, also. I told him I just had to spend more time with my family. But, here's the but, for a good cause we could have one Saturday night class a month.

I consciously knew I should have talked this over with my wife first. I went home and told Moni about our plan and asked, "What do you think, honey?" Oh, I, also, had told Moni we wanted to have a class on Christmas Eve. Moni looked at me and said, "I'll have to pray about it."

A couple of days later the chaplain called and asked if Steve and I had decided what to put on the schedule. I told him to pencil us in on the fourth Saturday of each month.

I went home that afternoon proud of my decision. I never gave a thought to how arrogant I was being and how hurt Moni might be. I proudly told her Steve and I decided to have a class on the fourth Saturday of the month and the first one was this weekend.

She blew a fuse! Her reply went something like this: The audacity of you to ask my approval and still do what you want. This seems too familiar; nothing has changed. You went to the prison on your son's birthday, and I guess you're going on Christmas Eve, too.

I knew I had messed up. I reminded Moni that D. J. wasn't even home on his birthday. Mrs. Jeri had called and needed to make the schedule. I played my trump card and told Moni that whenever she prayed and knew it was for the right reason, it was usually okay.

She said, "You didn't even give God time to answer. You just did it your way."

There are two parts to this story – my addictive behavior and Moni's codependent behavior. She is accustomed to having control of and making family decisions. She has had to. Most of the time she's been right. She's having trouble giving up control and letting go of all resentments.

She and I both knew I had good intentions. The situation was just handled poorly. I should have been more respectful to her feelings; she should have talked about her feelings before they became resentments. There was a definite lack of communication.

I knew I had unintentionally stepped over the line. I have this prayer: God, don't let me hurt anyone today. I truly and honestly do have this prayer in my heart. Yet I had hurt Moni.

I started wondering and worrying if I stopped my prison ministry, would I be all right? See, this ministry is so important to my own recovery. Have I learned enough? Am I strong enough to resist temptation on my own? What am I going to do? How can I make Moni understand?

The next morning Moni had an appointment at the hospital with her doctor. She called me and said, "I need to tell you just how aggravating God is."

I asked her what she meant. She proceeded to tell me how a guard brought two female inmates in shackles and chains into the waiting room, and God sat them down directly in front of her. She told me how sad and ashamed they looked. She said she knew they were hurting and she felt so bad for them. She then said, "Of course, I want you to go and go any eve you possibly can."

I thank God for giving me a wife that recognizes God. She could just as easily have resented these inmates and me if she had been as selfish as I.

I'M POWERLESS? HIGHER POWER?

STEPS 1 AND 2

Powerless? Not I! I can do this; I can stop any time I want. We realize we are powerless when we relate it to "one is too many and a thousand is not enough." The clinical theory behind this is it's only a mental obsession until we use that first time; then it becomes a craving. Most of us don't have enough will power to resist cravings. When the monkey gets on our backs, how do we get him off?

Well, what does this higher power mean? My first thought was God, but this became confusing, because I found we couldn't talk about Jesus at meetings. Too, I'm not sure I know or trust this God people talk about as being the one who sustains us. There were plenty of times I prayed, and nothing happened.

So I would find myself just holding on the only way I knew how. I knew nothing about letting go or surrendering. I was still trying to rely on my strength and will power which were ebbing fast. I started hearing "one day at a time," "let go and let God," and "fake it till you make it."

Desperately looking for relief since my old remedy for pain had stopped working, I began to realize I needed help with my addiction. It was time to check into a rehab clinic. I thought those folks could show me the way and this would be all I needed to straighten out my problems. This would be the last time I'd have to worry about addiction. I could get through this and be miserable no more.

I was taught to go to meetings – 90 days, 90 meetings. I'll try it. I went to meetings and would hear things I didn't think pertained to me. I thought this is not where I need to be, I have nothing in common with these people, there's nothing I can learn here. About the third day my mind began to clear somewhat, and a young man across the room began to talk about the misery he had experienced; he proceeded to tell MY story.

Everyday the meetings started with a prayer. Then they talked about the first three steps. "Come to believe in a Higher Power of your own understanding" really stood out to me. Also, in all my confusion I kept hearing "just for today." I thought I can handle this "just for today" bit; I'll learn it, know it and move on.

I knew about "baggage." We all have it. A friend asked, "With what do you struggle?" I struggled with my baggage becoming heavier and heavier but still struggled to carry it all by myself. I still had not surrendered. Up until now I had handled my life on my own. And look where I am!

I began to wonder what am I doing, why am I here, how did this happen? I have become slowly and painfully empty. Have I become powerless? I don't care about myself; how could anyone else care about me? Now I'm hopeless.

It was time to try God. I wanted to find out about this God who loves us all. I was skeptical because I had prayed and asked the Lord for help many times, but I was still addicted. I kept doing the things I didn't want to; it seemed I was incapable of doing what I knew was right. There seemed to be something in the way. It's I who was in the way. I'm in trouble when I try to handle my troubles and carry them alone. I have to surrender all.

Romans 7:18-20 says, "I know I'm rotten through and through. No matter which way I turn, I can't make myself do right. I want to but I can't. When I want to do good, I don't, and when I try not to do wrong, I do it anyway. But if I'm doing what I don't want to do, it's not me, it's my sinful nature."

Have you and I become miserable enough? "I'm miserable! Who will free me? Thank God, Jesus Christ our Lord" (Romans 7:24-25).

Recovery is not that easy. Salvation is free; everything else comes with a price. The most challenging part lies in developing and having a relationship with God. Allow him to show us and help us carry our baggage. If we weren't powerless to do it alone, we wouldn't be here. We wouldn't have a story to tell. If we push God away, we hold on to the past. The past is history, and history repeats itself.

IMPULSIVE BEHAVIOR

Secular programs teach that addicts or "speed freaks" have impulsive and compulsive behavior. Is it natural to have an irresistible urge to do something completely irrational?

Occasionally it may not be such a bad thing if we are people who live cautiously, always trying to avoid making bad choices and mistakes, to do something totally out of character. For those of us who struggle with a substance abuse problem, acting impulsively and compulsively can definitely lead to problems. Most likely, our impulsive and compulsive behavior developed early in life.

An example of impulsive behavior is picking up and purchasing something that looks intriguing while waiting in a checkout line. We don't think about the need or usefulness of the item. When we get home, we think, "I didn't need to spend my money on this I didn't need."

An example of compulsive behavior is attempting to assemble an item without reading the instructions. We get to a step and can't find a part. If we had followed the directions, we would have discovered the part was missing when we initially opened the package. Now we have to repackage the product and return it to the store.

Both these scenarios have negative outcomes. There is some level of insanity in repeating these behaviors over and over. An addict's behavior is characterized by both impulsive and compulsive behavior. Impulsive behavior is not premeditated; it's a spontaneous action caused by habitual action on our part. It's voluntary, free of outside influence. Compulsive behavior comes into play when we have the compulsion or need to change the way we feel at a moment's notice. We have a premeditated way of doing this.

There are times in recovery when we believe in our hearts we have mastered addiction and the recovery program. Then we find ourselves in a predicament. Our impulsive behavior will have us take a wrong short cut, for instance, into dangerous areas simply because we are not patient enough to go around the long way. We don't take time to evaluate the situation that could lead us into danger. Even in this scenario we can't wait for what we want. Our compulsive behavior will continue to take this route even when we have better directions from our peers in recovery. We have the inability to wait on gratification.

When we get restless, can't be still and lose patience, we then become anxious and even obsessive. Anxiety causes impulsive behavior, whether it is grabbing another purchase or driving in that familiar direction until, before we realize it, we're at the dope house. It is hard to control our thoughts and compulsions because we can already feel an intense euphoria, the rush we feel before we ever get the drugs in our hands.

Impulsive and compulsive behavior will both trip us up in recovery. Both can lead us back into active addiction. One of God's many promises says when we give our lives to him, He will make our weaknesses our strengths. "God is our refuge and strength, always ready to help in times of trouble. So we will not fear" (Psalm 46:1-2).

When we are tempted, we should "Be still and quiet and know that I am God" (Psalm 46:10). Matthew 26:41 says, "Keep alert and pray. Otherwise temptation will overpower you. For though the spirit is willing enough, the body is weak."

INSECURITY

People who have the nature or predisposition to become addicts are usually emotionally insecure. We base our self-worth on what we accomplish or what others think of us. At some point in recovery, we have to face the fact we can never do enough or be good enough to gain the approval of some people.

Failure gives us a complex, makes us believe we are worthless. There are times when we've failed because we were trying to accomplish the impossible, something that was simply out of our reach, something we neither had the gifts nor talents to do. When we fail repeatedly, our self-esteem has too many bruises. We feel an incredible amount of pain and then seek a way to escape this pain.

Feelings of insecurity and low self-esteem are painful; they weaken us. Our strength will come from addressing the underlying problem rather than focusing on ways to cover it up. The problem with the addict's solution is, while in the beginning the drugs did give us courage to say and do things, our actions were not part of our normal nature. Of course, our behavior under the influence works against us.

When we get into recovery, our battle to find security and significance has just begun. Most of us started so early in life we believe and accept that our past is who we are. We are deceiving ourselves. Somewhere near the end of active addiction, we begin to feel inadequate and have no confidence. Insecurity causes us to worry;

worry increases fear. In recovery we carry our insecurity, worry and fear with us.

We meet people who look and sound as if they have it together. We will never develop self-esteem if we compare our strengths and weaknesses to others. When we attempt to be like them, we put unreasonable expectations on ourselves. If we attempt to live up to another person's standards, failure is inevitable. Fear of failure will cause us to avoid and even resist the principles of recovery.

By committing to finding a connection in recovery that is effective and by focusing on that connection, our character will improve. Our talents and abilities will emerge. We will find our very own purpose.

Sharing our insecurities, worries and fears with others is effective in teaching, in helping others in recovery. Recovery is tough but rewarding if we are persistent.

What part does God play? Some of us may have had harsh, condemning or downright cruel, abusive mothers or fathers. Our perception of God, our father, may be hard and judgmental. Remember we are too sensitive and our feelings are distorted. We have a struggle with understanding, believing and trusting God. Our trust issues cause us to be uncertain and fearful of God, making our quest for a relationship difficult.

Every perception we have of God has a direct influence on how much we allow him to participate in our lives. Many of us have an unclear vision of God's grace and unconditional love. We can wrap our minds around what seems to be another concept of recovery, the God thing, but can or do we believe it in our hearts?

Our pasts tell us if we fail, God will not love us or, even worse, He will abandon us. We have to believe God's grace will forgive us and his love will never leave us. When we have feelings of insecurity, it is not of God. We lack the peace only He offers. God wants to set us free and make us secure. "Whosoever believes in me shall not perish but have everlasting life" (John3:16).

Society bases a person's importance on what that person knows or what he does. Isaiah 43:1 says, "I have redeemed you, I have called you by your name, you are mine." We should base ourselves on whom we are in Christ.

In Ephesians 1, God blessed all his people "with every spiritual blessing." Believers bless God by giving all power and glory to Him.

INTENSITY VS. INTIMACY

In the midst of our addictions and even before, we develop misconceptions about intensity and intimacy. In recovery we must be aware of their differences and not mistake or substitute one for the other.

Drugs change the way we think; we think only of ourselves. Drugs distort our feelings until we don't or can't recognize the difference between intensity and intimacy; we confuse the two. During active addiction we begin a relationship with another person. The drugs already give us pleasure; the relationship gives us pleasure. We have a misconception about our feelings. Actually, we can't distinguish between the intensity of our feelings and intimacy. We mistake the intensity of sexual experiences for the intimacy that is developed only through a nurturing partnership with someone.

Sex is a natural activity intended by God to be shared in love between two people, a man and a woman. The intensity of sex should not be mistaken for love. Love is as love does. Love takes work and courage specifically directed towards the spiritual growth of partners.

One of the reasons we choose to use drugs is control. We know what we will get from our choice of drug. With people and relationships, there is no certainty. When we expect one thing and get another, we develop resentments. In relationships we can not control the other person. Being self-centered and selfish instead of waiting, having patience and control of ourselves, we choose the substance over the person. We actually begin and choose to have a relationship with drug addiction and become intimate with addiction alone.

Relationships are important in recovery, but we must be ever wary of any situation so we don't confuse actions as intimacy. Be cautious not to confuse the intensity of someone's actions, such as buying us nice things or entertaining us, with love. While these things are exciting, they are not intimate.

We can not cure our human problems with nonhuman intervention. But being spoiled or at least sheltered from an early age, this is what most of us have come to expect. Anytime something bad happened, some codependent person would intervene to save us from feeling pain. The only way that person knew was to entertain us. In reality this stunted our emotional growth, not allowing us to learn to cope with disappointments. This illustrates how we learned to use intensity and avoid intimacy.

Some of us began using at such an early age we never experienced much adherence to intimacy. Our lives have been based on intensity, and we must recognize our behavior will always be attracted to intensity.

Going through life with this behavior, always seeking instant gratification, we continue to manipulate every situation. But at some point, our drugs stop working. Then the consequences of our actions get serious; they are larger than we are capable of handling on our own. In desperation we make that 911 call to God. Because of our behavior being what it is, we expect some intense spiritual intervention. There is no doubt "God can do all things." He is the great interventionist.

In Psalms 37, He tells us to not fret, trust in him, commit our ways and wait patiently for him. God says in Luke 9:23, "Pick up your cross daily and follow me." "We can do all things through Christ who strengthens us" (Philippians 4:13).

Even with all God's directions, recovery is hard to grasp. We can't understand and comprehend how to just stop and be still. We think recovery, like everything else in our lives, should be intense – hurry up and get it done! The fact is we have to be diligent in our works to transform our hearts and minds.

In another sense, our intensity can work for us. Our energy, concentration and determination are all intense. If we search for answers with all our energy, concentrate on a solution and stay determined to succeed, recovery is possible.

INTENTIONS

What are our intentions? Are they honorable? Or do we always have an ulterior motive? During active addiction we make plans but never seem to follow through; these plans always come secondary to our drug use. Our intentions are good but useless.

Scripture refers to intentions of the heart. If recovery is in our hearts, why do we continually make selfish, self-centered choices? Drug addiction has such a strong-hold; it controls our every thought to the point everything seems hopeless. None of us have intentions of hurting loved ones or making them and ourselves miserable. Our intent was never to isolate ourselves and render everyone helpless. We never intended to speak disrespectfully to others. We didn't intend to do a lot of the things we did.

There are times, in moments of clarity, we have the motivation to seek recovery. Maybe it's because we become "sick and tired of being sick and tired." For some of us it may be the consequences of our actions. We have intentions of committing to rehab and recovery, to attending meetings and church, to having accountability and to and the list goes on and on.

Recovery takes work. We often fail because of our laziness to do the work. Due to our low self-esteem, we often feel we don't fit in recovery either. Usually our unconscious intentions are to discredit recovery. Our arrogance tells us we're more intelligent; our pride tells us we don't need help; our denial tells us we're not that bad; our fear tells us we may be ridiculed.

Then we run out of resources and are forced into recovery. Our intentions then are to get those people off our backs. We make an attempt to learn the right things to say and do, to look as if we've got this. Addiction has no honor. If our intentions are not honorable, we will fail. If we truly want to beat addiction, our intentions must become desires of the heart.

It's easy to show good intentions when we are in the box - in church with Christians, in rehab where we have supervision and accountability. Jailhouse religion is almost a must, the only peace and comfort we know. We call out to God and make promises in dark times and have every intention of keeping these promises. Really? What are our true intentions? Is it to only appear that our behavior has changed? Sadly for some, this is the case. For many of us, we want to keep our word, our promises. Yet by nature we are selfish.

So, are our intentions for self or for the glory of God? Desires or intentions of the heart are great searchlights for whom we have become. When recovery begins in our hearts, God resides inside us; God is love and love conquers all things. Each day ask yourself, what are my intentions? Be still for just a moment before making decisions and make them honorable before God.

I challenge you to pray something like this:

> God, don't let me hurt anyone today. Help me know my intentions are to honor you and not myself. Let my actions be for your glory. My wish is to answer your calling and purpose for me. I pray that I wake each morning living and loving as Jesus does, to serve people in a manner that is pleasing to you. I thank you that your desire is for my salvation. Amen.

I'VE GOT IT!

Steve and I have a ministry on Wednesday nights at the Bleckley PDC. I often make an almost cruel joke and ask, "What have y'all been doing today?" Evelyn, one of our girls, always smiles and answers, "Time," then laughs. You see, Evelyn has found her peace with God; she is content to be still and listen for his answers to lead her in what lies ahead.

In recovery how and when do we know we've "got it?" Is it after a certain amount of time passes? How do we how when we've changed? We know change challenges us to grow. Do our changes bring us successes? We must be wary of success; success can breed arrogance. We want others to be proud of us; we tend to use all kinds of inspirational metaphors to impress them. Could we be viewing the word through rose colored glasses?

Bouncing back physically can deceive us and give us a false sense of security, especially if we are not completely prepared mentally and spiritually. Typically a minute step for us seems to be a huge success. We tend to get overly confident, and we become complacent. We don't put recovery first.

When we begin to feel some change, we expect others to immediately recognize it, too. We expect them to react in a certain way. When they don't, we feel hurt or angry. We are setting ourselves up for a relapse. So do we have this? Are we trained, equipped and able?

In Bible study, I learned about Shamgar, a farmer in the book of Judges. He went to war to defend Israel. He killed six hundred Philistines with no weapons, only his farm tools. He had no training, only God's guidance. He, also, became the third Judge of Israel. The moral of this story is start where you are, use what you have and do what you can.

It's in our nature to dream and make selfish plans and then ask God to bless them. It's not natural to be still, ask and then wait on his plan. Today I have stopped using as a solution for my troubles. I'm working on recovery, but I can't say, "I've got it."

"I am not saying I have reached perfection, but I am working toward that day when I finally am all that Christ Jesus saved me to be. I am still not all I should be, but I'm focusing on forgetting the past and looking forward to what lies ahead" (Philippians 3:12-14). When I meet Jesus at the gates of heaven, I can say, "I've got it!"

JUDGMENTAL

Most people are judgmental. For those of us who have faults, and we all do, we look for people who exhibit worse behavior to compare ourselves to. Finding their shortcomings somehow justifies our own. We will say to ourselves, "Their problem is worse, so I'm not so bad."

Most of us will criticize a person instead of helping them. In Galatians 6:12 we learn it is a responsibility to gently and humbly help a person who is overcome by sin to get back on the right path. Of course, we need to get ourselves on the right path first. Matthew 7:3 says, "Why worry about a speck in your friend's eye when you have a log in your own."

Scripture, also, says we are hypocrites when we judge before cleaning up our own lives. It's human nature to point a finger at others when we're caught doing wrong. Blaming others for fault and failure is avoiding the issues in our own behavior. We continue to blame others and take moral inventory of people in order to measure the good and bad in ourselves.

We must stop and take inventory of our own lives. Our pitfalls in addiction have caused us to avoid feeling sorrow. This is why recovery is so painful. We must confront the causes of our pain to be released from our guilt and shame.

We find ourselves dwelling on our failures and define them as faults in our character. Trying to overcome these defects is so overwhelming, we become discouraged with our progress or lack thereof and begin to measure our success by the failure in others. This is being lazy, failing to work to change. No one ever said recovery was easy!

We must constantly exercise self examination and stop blaming and judging others. Many times people in our lives have taken the blame for us; they did this trying to help us. It's time we accepted the blame. Jesus said, "You are all at fault, but I'll take the blame."

Yes, we are all guilty, if not for the obvious, then for judging others to validate our own shortcomings. In recovery there will come a time when we "get it" and take responsibility for our own actions and lives. Stop blaming and judging. Own up! It'll set you free.

JUST SAY NO!

Many of us have a problem with "no." Early on in life we may have had acceptance issues. We tend to try our best to please everyone by saying yes to things we know are wrong, things we shouldn't do and things we don't even want to do.

Becoming people pleasers can become very uncomfortable and tiresome. We end up doing for others; there is no time and nothing rewarding for ourselves.

I once was asked by a counselor friend of mine if I knew anyone who was in the market for a saddle. Immediately, I said, "I'll buy it." Wow! I didn't even have a horse.

Then there was the time I bought a box of rifle cartridges. I then had to go and purchase a rifle for them. In both cases my judgment was irrational – you could probably say crazy.

Going back to the saddle story – I thought the guy selling the saddle needed the money and I could help. My thought was I could buy a horse and board it until I could buy a farm and build a barn and pen. Then I would have time to ride it. Maybe if I obligated money towards a horse, feed and a farm, I would then spend my time chasing a wild horse instead of drugs.

Back to saying "no" – I spoke with my dad who, also, has a terrible time saying "no." It's hard to say "no" when helping/serving others. We have a need in our lives to honor God with service work. But we addicts must always remember the selfishness in addiction. Is saying yes or no for me and my benefit only? Shawn, a friend and accountability partner in my addictive behavior group, reminded me of a very important fact, a spiritual fact. Your first ministry is at home. Consider your family first.

Many times saying yes is the right thing to do. But did I say yes because it was the right thing or because of the recognition I would receive? Did I have an agenda?

Recently my wife and I had a very trying situation. We found ourselves taking care of a cancer patient who had no family within the state. He had to have 24/7 care, and we were two of maybe a half dozen people he knew and the only ones he wanted by his side.

I lived with him for seven weeks. This was the only time I had slept apart from my family in 23 years except for rehab. It was a trying time for our faith. We couldn't help but ask, "Why us, Lord?" It was hard keeping up two households. It became exhausting with us keeping our everyday schedules, making his appointments and sitting at the hospital and so on.

Could we have said "no?" Of course, we could; our church family would have helped. Actually, this turned out to be a blessing for us and this friend. Along with our pastor Ken and a few of our friends, we had the opportunity to exhibit a kind of love to this man he had never experienced. He expressed to me how we had a great group of friends and how he felt so much love during this time in his life. It was, also, a time our children sacrificed in the name of love and God.

Saying yes was the right thing to do. God blessed us all during this time. But we do have to realize there are times we can't do it all; we have to ask others for help. We often think we are the only ones who can get the job done. Not so!

In recovery there has to be a change. We have to break the habit of agreeing and always saying "yes." The change for me is thinking things through, considering all prior obligations and putting my family first.

Of course, I know that God's will comes first – God, then family. Sometimes saying "no" is the right thing to do.

Matthew 6:33 says, "Seek first the kingdom of God and his righteousness, and all these things shall be added to you."

"Do not be conformed to this world, but be transformed by the receiving of your mind, that you may prove what is that good and acceptable and perfect will of God" (Romans 12:2).

KNOWING

Have you ever heard "you know what you know because you just know it?" There is a time in our addiction when we begin to think that life sucks. Our own life really sucks, and we just have to live with it. Our only thoughts are how bad our circumstances are, how someone in our life has caused all our anguish and how we can get the relief we need.

Then somehow there is some kind of intervention. Something significant happens; we gain a minute amount of control over our addiction or at least for a while it is being controlled for us.

While being stopped in our tracks, we have time to ponder our situation and learn about addiction. We discover we were not bad people; we are people with a tremendous amount of mental and emotional pain for which we have chosen the wrong solution for dealing with it for far too long.

Those of us who manage to stay clean for a long enough period of time are blessed to explore and manage our emotions and behavior and to gain a better understanding about our compulsion to change the way we feel. Most of us, though, get to a point where we begin to feel better, our physical health is improved and we learn a little about recovery, mostly with the idea being "just don't pick up and use drugs." Then we think and even say, "I've got this."

Recently a great friend and spiritual leader made this statement: "I don't know." This man has a theology degree and has been a pastor for ten years. He teaches, preaches and sings; he's a musical evangelist. Yet when you ask him his title or what he likes to be called, he merely says, "I'd rather you call me Jon and refer to me as a student of God." He continues to explain why he says I don't know.

If we say we know something or know all we need to know, we shut the door on change and progress. We close our hearts and minds to growth and maturity. We put on blindfolds when we say this is the way things are and the way they will stay. We are unwilling to see things any other way. We may be afraid of change.

When we make the decision to close our minds to knowledge, we then become unteachable. Many of us think we are more intelligent than the teacher, but usually the teacher has the most experience.

Following our unteachable arrogance is complacency where we remove ourselves from all our support and accountability. Complacency is that place where we think we know all we need to know and are not interested in anything anyone has to say even if it's valuable to our health in recovery. After we have become comfortable and satisfied in our complacency, we get careless.

Being careless takes us to risky places where we are tempted and influenced by people who can be dangerous to us. Our recklessness gets us into positions where our vision is blurred. We then begin to justify "one" as being okay and rationalize how we deserve it.

Now, if we claim to know all about addiction and what to do about it, we are saying we are a know-it-all. Webster's dictionary says this is one having or reflecting intelligence or one who is cognizant and has knowledge of something through personal experience. This is what we want people to think. My wife can set me straight; she often reminds me she can't hear what I am saying because my actions are too loud.

So if we are so intelligent and knowledgeable, why do we still make such bad choices? Is it the lack of commitment or our arrogance? Is the pain too great? Have we shut the door on our own growth and maturity in recovery by saying "I know, I've got this?" If by saying "I don't know" and not giving up on finding the answers, change in us will occur.

Recovery comes not by what we know but what we seek out of recovery itself. Faith comes by hearing not from what we have heard. Faith believes in the invisible while making it visible. Faith is believing and hope is where we can see ourselves in the future.

"Now faith is the assurance of things hoped for and the evidence of things not seen" (Hebrews 11:1). Don't shut the door on recovery!

KNOWING THE RIGHT THINGS TO SAY

Do I say all the right things for my benefit or for those I think want to hear them? The right things or good stuff includes the terminology, psychobabble and NA and AA terms. Do I really and truly mean what I say? Do I practice what I preach? When I'm talking, do I even hear what I'm saying?

I want people to be proud of me; do I learn all this to impress the one's who ask questions or are my intentions to mislead everyone? I want people at meetings to think I'm really working the program when I recite the 12 steps, the traditions and Just for Today. I can read them, write them, recite them, but do I practice the principles in my life and actually work the steps? I've been told over and over to try it, it really works.

Am I talking or walking?

We don't always have an agenda when we're talking the talk. Normally we have good intentions to do the right thing. But when we don't, we still use the talk to try to cover our backsliding.

Are we just being people pleasers and, at the same time, trying to get everyone off our backs? What do you think when someone "blows you smoke" and you know it? How does it make you feel? I sometimes get all arrogant and say, "Wait a minute; you're talking to the master of deception. You can't shit a shitter."

Do we have any remorse or a conscience when we lie? Do we

realize we have just lost our accountability with this person? My Uncle Hudson said, "I don't really mind someone lying to me; I just mind it when he expects me to believe it."

For me, I have to remember I'm not the judge. I am only responsible for the truth and presenting God's word. God represents the truth. It doesn't matter what others think when I saying what they want to hear. What matters is having a conscience and not lying. If doesn't matter if others know you're lying; you know it and God knows it.

We need to have the right intentions and use our knowledge in positive ways. I have to tell my family sometimes that I wasn't getting stupid, I was making bad choices. Now if I use wisdom and share this knowledge, I can grow and those around me can benefit. This will mean I'm making good decisions and being careful of others' feelings.

We are only responsible for the truth, not for what others think or do with our witnessing. Don't loose or misuse what we have! Stay focused! In Proverbs 4:20-27 we read

> Don't lose sight of my words. Let them penetrate deep within your heart, for they will bring life and radiant health to anyone who discovers their meaning.
> Above all else, guard your heart, for it affects everything you do.
> Avoid all perverse talk; stay far from corrupt speech.
> Look straight ahead, and fix your eyes on what lies ahead of you.
> Mark out a straight path and stay safe.
> Don't get sidetracked; keep your feet from following evil.

"Keep a good conscience so that the thing you are slandered for and the people that mock your good behavior in Christ will be put to shame" (1 Peter 3:16). "It is necessary to be under authority, not only because of wrath (anger) but, also, for conscience sake" (Romans 13:5).

LAZINESS

There is a time to pray and a time to act. We should stop trying to be so spiritual when it's time to do something. Get up and participate instead of waiting for someone to tell you what to do.

We must all pursue basic healthy lifestyles. This includes eating healthy, engaging in fun activities which involve family and friends and staying persistent in attending our recovery classes and meetings. Not taking care of ourselves physically leads to a lack of motivation. Then we let ourselves become disconnected; this leads to a deprivation of emotional support. We get lazy and risk our recovery.

When we have wronged someone, we must not delay reconciling as soon as possible to avoid any resentments materializing that will hinder our recovery. It's natural to want to procrastinate when things in our lives become tough. It's easy to put off doing anything about problems when they arise. We get discouraged when the going gets hard. The longer we put off correcting a problem, the more consequences we have to face and the more we suffer.

In addiction we get to the point we think our lives can not be changed. Truth is it's never too late to begin recovery. In the beginning of recovery, we find ourselves full of anger, resentment, hatred, guilt, shame, etc. When we're lazy and put off using the principles in recovery, our hearts begin to harden. Making excuses long enough lessens our ability to hear God's voice.

We are accountable for our attitudes and actions. We try to keep doing things our way. Procrastinating until the problem gets out of hand leads us closer towards destruction.

To find a balance in our lives, relationships, work and even pleasure, we have to put each one in perspective. This can only be done through a relationship with God. Sometimes we make promises to God like our 911 prayers: "God, if you'll help me through this one, I'll do anything you want." We shouldn't make these promises and take God for granted. God is not an enabler. God does for us what we can not do for ourselves; he then leaves the rest up to us.

When we are in a serious situation or a dangerous place, it's not time to be spiritual; it's time to get up and leave. God provides a path; we have to take the steps. That's not to say we always know what to do. Sometimes it's acting on faith; it's hearing God's voice inside. When we know what God wants us to do and we procrastinate, this is disobedience. Doing it tomorrow should not be mistaken for obedience. Sitting around and saying God will provide is an excuse for being lazy. Many of our struggles are the consequences of our procrastination.

While in recovery we gain strength through trials. Our support comes from our peers in our programs, groups and churches. Complacency comes from success in recovery. We begin to think we "have it" and the more we procrastinate, the closer we progress towards failure. What if Noah had procrastinated? God told Noah he had a certain amount of time to build the ark. When it was time to shut the door, nothing else could board.

We can not be stable in recovery until we make carrying the message of hope to others who suffer. This is a necessary part of recovery. "Therefore encourage one another and build each other up, just as you are doing" (1 Thessalonians 5:11). "Seek the Lord while he may be found; call on him while He is close" (Isaiah 55:6).

Read Revelations 22:10.

LETTING GO

How much junk in our hearts and minds can we let go and put behind us? How and why did this happen to me; what do I do about it? First and foremost we have to decide drugs can no longer be our solution to our problems. Let the drugs go!

We have a lot of pride. Pride can be the greatest enemy of the mind. Our pride tells us we can not ask for help, we can do it on our own or we've got this. This leads to arrogance. We know all the answers; we can fool people; we can beat the system. Let this pride and arrogance go!

Control is another of our downfalls. What can we control? Usually we can not control much at all. When we try to control, we end up manipulating others. Control and manipulation are very selfish; we put our wants and needs above those who care about us. Let control and manipulation go!

Resentments are must hurtful to our own hearts. Some resentments are created by others; these are out of our control. We have to realize resentments only hurt us. More times than not, the other party neither knows nor cares how we feel.

Resentments come from our expectations of others. It has been said the definition of expectation is a premeditated resentment. If he doesn't do what I want the way I want it, I'm going to be mad. So when we have expectations of others and harbor bad feelings, they become resentments; they hinder our hearts from healing and recovery. Let resentments go!

After having a spiritual awakening, we start seeing our past as bad and begin to feel guilty; we're ashamed. Then we worry. We worry about what someone thinks of us; we worry about things at home, our spouses, our children. Let the worry go!

Put all this behind you! Spend this time with yourself and with God. Let the past go! We can't fix it. Work on forgiving yourself. This is a long list and a tall order to do all at once. Remember, easy does it. Addiction didn't happen in a day, neither will recovery. Take one thing at a time, one day at a time together with God.

Let go of self; stop fighting. In 2 Timothy 4:7-8, Jesus said he had already fought the fight for us.

The glass half full or half empty is a great analogy. We as addicts can only see the glass half empty. The glass will never be full until we put something in it. We have to give back instead of taking. Matthew 12:43-45 says, "When an evil spirit leaves a person, it goes to the desert looking for a rest and finding none, it says, 'I will return to the person I came from.' It returns to the house and finds it clean and empty. Then the spirit finds seven more spirits even more evil than itself who move in with that person and live there." That person is worse off than ever.

We think we can just clean up and let go; that's all we have to do. We still have obsessive thoughts and are starving emotionally. Sometimes it seems impossible to stop thinking of what filled that empty place. We have to fill that clean and empty house. We fill it with the word of God. Let go and let God!

How? Trust! We trust God and believe in His word. His words will change our thoughts and fill our hearts. "For I know the plans I have for you. They are plans for good, not disaster, to give you a future and a hope" (Jeremiah 29:11).

LIVING IN THE PAST

As children, life was easy with very few cares, concerns or responsibilities. For the most part the past was much easier than the present with our responsibilities, home life, parenting, bills, etc. As life evolves, so do we into adulthood. Then something devastating happened that was serious enough to detour us from the natural progression of life.

As our health, relationships and livelihood decline, we begin to blame everyone but ourselves for our shortcomings. As addicts the progression of addiction worsens as we try to escape the pain from our past. This painful past hinders our recovery. We are totally responsible for most of our problems. Some problems are misconstrued because of our perception of what happened and who was to blame.

The past causes us to hold grudges and have resentments which many times turn into anger and then conflict. Unforgiveness makes the past our present. The inability to forgive ourselves, also, makes the past current.

Living in the past makes us doubt that life will ever be any better; we believe we will never succeed. Putting ourselves down reinforces failure. We place unnecessary attention and energy on everything that goes wrong.

Addiction has taken so much of our time and energy that we have failed in most areas of our lives. We harp on our failures. If we continue thinking this way, we will eventually believe we are only as good as our failures and deserve even less.

I have a friend who says I, at times, am very critical of myself. His concern brings to my attention the fact that I am still in recovery. As a recovering addict, I am still quite sensitive and carry a tremendous amount of guilt and shame for the dysfunctional things of which I was part that created pain and suffering for those I love. I simply say I am sensitive to the fact I made a mess out of my life. That's okay. We do not want to forget the past, but we should not dwell on it, just learn from it.

In recovery we do have to explore the past. We have to face the pain that caused our addiction and the pain we created for ourselves. Recovery is also painful. That's why it is so important to 'live just for today' and make a decision to 'accept life on life's terms.' Life owes us nothing! Growth and maturity rely on our determination to change our behavior in the future.

Jesus paid the ultimate sacrifice for our sins. "He is so rich in kindness that he purchased our freedom (redemption) through the blood of his son and our sins are forgiven" (Ephesians 1:7).

In Haggai 2 God speaks of rebuilding the temple and He says consider your ways. "Is there anyone who can remember this house – the temple – as it was before? In comparison how does it look now?" (Haggai 2:3). "The future glory of this temple will be greater than its past glory, says the Lord. And to this place I will bring peace" (Haggai 2:9). The temple is YOU.

Psalm 107:2 says, "Let the redeemed of the Lord say so."

LOOK AT ME!

Have you ever thought you were the center of the universe and the world revolved around you? Most of us have or had parents or loved ones who made us feel this way. I asked my wife this question and she said only as a child. My wife has never had an alcohol or drug problem; her only addiction has been me.

Soon after we begin using drugs, our mental and emotional growth and maturity stop; we think as a child. At first we get an euphoric feeling that increases our performance. Feeling good about ourselves, we are the life of the party. We perform a little too much, show out and occasionally embarrass ourselves.

In general we're successful in life. We may even do something outstanding. Then we get all blown up over our success and, either consciously or subconsciously, think look at me, look at how smart and successful I am. We tend to become arrogant after succeeding over and over again without failure.

We begin to think we can do drugs successfully with no consequences, as though we are above the law or are smarter than those who get caught. The vision we want to project is look at me, I'm different.

Early on in recovery, we think this should not take too long. Our health is improving, and we're feeling better physically. We get into meetings, learn some terminology and learn all the right things to say. We feed off each other's ideas and concerns; this is why being together, having a network and combining and compiling information is effective. Then we begin to think maybe we're smarter than our fellow addicts. We try to impress others with our wit or by downplaying the seriousness of our situation. We subtly insinuate we know all there is to know. Some of us learn to quote the steps of recovery and even Bible verses. We're saying, "Look at me."

The truth is this is our cover; our performance is actually hiding what's going on inside us. If we have to perform or tell people how good we're doing, most likely we are not doing too well.

We always have an agenda. We use and intrude on others, expecting them to be there for us no matter where or when. We have this misconception about sacrifice. In our minds when we are going through tough times, we feel we are sacrificing. We feel that since we've sacrificed, others owe us something back. What do they owe us? Our loved ones have already sacrificed enough due to the guilt trips we lay on them. They owe us nothing. What they do give us now comes from love only.

Recovery comes at a cost with a lot of patience and hard work. It is a process of getting honest, identifying pain and taking responsibility for our recovery. The secular programs use the word 'baffling' concerning the behavior of addiction. Our pride and arrogance will lead us to believe, we alone can accomplish this. We don't need God's help. Pride, also, hinders us from seeing and admitting what God sees in us. Only God can see the fear inside. It takes faith in God to recover.

Matthew 14:22-29 tells the story of Jesus walking on water. Everyone is afraid; Peter says if you are the son of God, let me walk to you. Jesus told Peter to come and Peter did. Peter had to let go of his fears and have faith to succeed. At the moment he looked back at the other disciples to say 'look at me,' he took his eyes off Jesus. We can't become careless or complacent; the 'look at me' attitude only ensures relapse. Keep your eyes on the Lord.

LOSS/GRIEF

Everyone experiences loss at some point. How we deal with that loss can and will affect us for the rest of our lives. Will we be bitter or better?

The closer the person was to us the more deeply we feel that loss. Knowing we are extra sensitive already, it's important not to perceive this loss as our fault – that we caused this, or this wouldn't have happened if we had done things differently. Accept the fact you had no control over this.

Some people deal with loss by just ignoring it. Others harp on it and use it as an excuse for their own bad behavior. It is so important to recognize the loss and deal with it. We will then grieve and grow.

Using loss in a healthy perspective can cause insight and understanding. The only way to move forward is to face it. The grief process is not a time for us to feel sorry for ourselves but to actually deal with our loss.

Grieving is necessary. We need to mourn; we need to feel and express sorrow. We need to grieve. It is painful. Research says it can take one to three years to deal with a significant loss.

Losses during active addiction have less emotional effect on us, because our ability to feel has been numbed by the drugs. We may not even be able to experience any emotion yet. People suffer in different ways and to different degrees. Don't judge!

Grief has many stages. Denial or shock comes first. We try to comprehend what has happened but may not experience any emotion yet.

The second is release; emotion is shown. Many times it's in the form of anger; we place blame. We even get angry with God; He let this happen. We feel sorry for ourselves, for the pain we are suffering. We feel we've lost everything. We then deal with guilt. What could I have done to prevent this?

The next stage is acceptance. We reorganize our lives and accept the loss. We fill our time with new relationships or by reconnecting with healthy people who can help us through the tough times.

When we are truly in recovery, we learn to feel and express our pain without avoiding or denying it. The bottom line is everyone has loss and grief. There is nothing that makes the grieving process easy.

True healing comes from acknowledging the loss and going through the grieving process. The greatest truth is God never leaves us; He travels this road with us.

We must know in our hearts no matter how big the loss or what the circumstances, there is a greater plan for our lives with God in control.

MATURITY AND SPIRITUAL GROWTH

We all go through fair weather and storms, successes and failures. It's how we handle victory and defeat that shows our character and our maturity as Christians.

We can't keep what we have without giving it away. Hebrews 12 -14 reads

> You have been Christians for a long time now, and you ought to be teaching others. Instead you need someone to teach you again the basic things a beginner must learn about the scriptures. We are like babies who only drink milk and cannot eat solid food. A person who lives on milk isn't far along in Christian life and doesn't know much about doing what is right. Solid food is for those who are mature, who have trained themselves to recognize the difference in right and wrong and then do what is right.

Chapter 6 of Hebrews tells us to stop going over the basics of Christianity again and again, to go on and become mature in our understanding. Surely we don't need to start over again with the importance of turning away from evil deeds and placing our faith in God.

Again, we are called to build the kingdom. Through storms, failure and even death we must keep our faith and hope to see ourselves grow.

When we come through the other side clean, we have matured. We should share how we fight through storms, look at failure as growth and forgive death.

If we are 'using,' we don't feel the pain. If we don't feel the pain, we are not maturing.

MISUNDERSTOOD

Addicts make lots of excuses, but the truth is, many times, we're misunderstood. We're not always trying to hurt and manipulate others. Fact is most of us are sensitive people and wouldn't intentionally hurt anyone. We carry around a ton of guilt and shame we wouldn't wish on anyone.

It's also a misconception that addicts can just quit at any time. By the time we've become chemically dependent on the drugs, it's virtually impossible for us to stop on our own. Everyone says we have a choice – to use or not to use. Actually, for an active addict there is no choice. We can't function without the drugs. Studies have shown something has to happen.

We need to go back to the beginning and explore the source of our pain. We'll usually find our temperament is too sensitive and we suffer from poor self-esteem. We tend to take responsibility for everything that happens whether it's our fault or not.

If temperament is the source, can our problem be genetic? Or is the problem environmental or learned behavior? Actually, it's both. We didn't have a choice in our genetic makeup or in how and where we were raised. Actually, no one does. Addicts just weren't strong enough to fight the negatives in their lives.

The programs tell us drugs and alcohol will lead to three things – jails, institutions and death. These are mere consequences. Yes, they are severe consequences, but, sadly, they don't stop us. People think if someone lost his job, home, family and possessions, he'd turn himself around. Regrettably, this doesn't stop our addiction. It just adds more pain we need to kill.

The secular programs call it the disease of addiction. My accountability partner and friend is a psychologist. He believes whole heartedly in the disease theory, relating to me addicts don't choose this life.

The programs have scientific studies that can back up their theories. They say addiction is a genetic disorder passed down from parent to child. This gene has not been identified yet.

The secular programs, also, believe in having a spiritual awakening. I believe it takes medical intervention and God to beat addiction.

So how do I change? I have to change my behavior, the way I think and act. Have you heard of the "dry drunk?" That's the addict who gets clean but still has an angry, bad attitude about everything. Many would say he was better when he was using or perhaps this is the real person, one we don't like.

When an addict gets off drugs, that person is only clean, not sober. Sobriety comes from working daily on our behavior, changing the way we do things and having peace of mind. We have to make a choice each day – do I want to hurt the people in my life any longer? We have to ask God for his help each day.

The secular programs speak of a higher power, a god of your own understanding. Remember drugs and alcohol have really messed up our thinking. We think those who loved us and tried to help us were against us. We're mad at God, because we prayed to Him for relief and He gave none. We go to programs looking for relief, not God. I know I did.

When the program spoke of a higher power, I was confused. The consensus was this higher power could be anything that works for you. The message was whatever works, just don't use or drink. The higher power that worked for me is God.

The God I serve today is the one that gives us the peace that surpasses all understanding, the living God, the only God who can set us free from the bondage of addiction. John 14:6 says, "I am the way, the truth and the life."

John and Bill, the authors of Alcoholics Anonymous, use the term higher power. The program was written for the sole purpose of recovery for everyone. Most come to the program looking for relief, not necessarily looking for God. But have no misunderstanding, their higher power is God. Their program was set up to introduce God slowly.

Only through trusting and believing in God can we recovering addicts find a real life. He will give us peace.

A MORAL DISEASE

Recently there was a tragic loss of life in our community. This loss touched my heart as well as the hearts of many others. There have been many different reactions to this death. This death was due to alcohol and drug addiction.

Some feel disgust, thinking she got what she deserved. Some feel guilty, thinking they failed her. Some feel guilt because they were embarrassed by her. Many feel a sense of relief, knowing her fight was over and she didn't have to struggle any longer. Some are taking the death personally and are angry or hurt. Most are just confused about why she just didn't "get it."

For those on the outside, addiction is hard to understand. There is the debate between teachers, counselors, therapists and researchers as to whether addiction is a moral issue or a disease. The moral theory says addiction is a behavior or sin problem. The disease theory says addiction is uncontrollable.

If in fact it is a moral issue, we do make choices and have the option to change our behavior. The disease theory says once we have it, we can not change it. I can not and will not discredit either theory. Both are valid and valuable to recovery.

ABC believes emotions and behavior are the catalysts for the beginning of our use and the reason for our relapse. At this point in my life in sobriety, it would be a very selfish moral decision to turn my back on my loved ones and begin using drugs again. Once I inject the drug, the craving for more begins, and the disease of addiction takes control because I can't stop it on my own. Medical research and technology have proven this theory to the extent we at least have to consider it and believe there is enough truth in it to stay in recovery and avoid relapse. Some people misunderstand why we do what we do; some have no tolerance left and just give up on us. The moral concept or theory appears a more sensible and legitimate understanding for many people. It is this concept that has worked for me in sobriety.

I have a close friend who is, also, my Bible study partner. He is struggling with why our friend had to die from addiction. We know she knew God and had an understanding of God's love and mercy. We recovering addicts have a responsibility. My friend believes at some point we must be accountable for our actions and make a commitment to recovery. We have an obligation to ourselves and our families to stop the madness. We are responsible for our behavior. In the same sense, we should make a commitment to God to be accountable to Him. With a new purpose in our hearts, we have an obligation to witness to others about God's mercy and redemption for us. There was and is an ongoing argument about whether we do this out of love for ourselves, others or God. Why can't it be all three?

Because of our independent, sinful and rebellious nature, we are not comfortable with and don't even like the words commitment, responsibility, accountability and obligation. But when we found ourselves in the depths of active addiction, we realized we couldn't depend on ourselves much less anyone else depending on us. We learned from the past we had to commit to something.

When using this terminology and speaking of God in the same context, it almost seems like it takes "works" to be in God's grace. It is my understanding we cannot work our way into heaven. It is, also, my belief we are responsible, have an obligation, should make a commitment to Christ and should be glad to be accountable to God because we love Him, not because we owe Him anything in return. We have to be responsible and pick up our cross daily. We have an obligation to do our part in building His kingdom.

"Become complete. Be of good comfort, be of one mind, live in peace; and the God of love and peace will be with you" (2 Corinthians 13:11).

"I am the way, the truth, and the life. No one comes to the Father except through me" (John 14:6).

OPTIONS

What are our options? Webster says an option is a choice, a selection, an act or opportunity of choosing. Choice suggests the opportunity or privilege of choosing freely.

When we get to what seems the end of our rope, we have a choice to make. We can continue our old behavior which leads to misery and destruction, or we have the option to recover.

In recovery there are important steps that have to be taken. The first is admitting there is a problem. Secondly, we must be humble and ask for help. This is tough to do because of the little pride we may still have left. But after enough pain, we can muster up some courage, find a little humility in our desperation and make an attempt at a new way of life.

We discover very quickly we have little understanding of the honesty required of us. Our arrogance tells us we have the option of telling just enough to appease people instead of readily and completely admitting our wrongs. Then there is our pain. We can't quite envision sharing this pain with others, especially a bunch of strangers who will see our fears and recognize our weaknesses and character defects.

In recovery we are taught it is imperative to change people, places and things. It is hard to abandon our old friends, familiar places and things. In the past, this is where we found our comfort. Addiction is very cunning. So we hang on to options. We will consciously stay away from the obvious and most dysfunctional people and places.

How many of us fail to cut ties with all of our past, like those "using" friends and connections only we know?

The choice here is whether to get completely honest with ourselves or not? Sometimes our lack of complete honesty is not evident even to the closest of our accountability partners. Sometimes our greatest danger is quite near. It could be a relative who "uses" with no consequences or one who may have prescription medicine but has no understanding of its danger for us. We have to be open in a successful recovery. We can not afford to keep secrets as an option.

Getting rid of and stopping the use of drugs are first and foremost important to recovery. It is necessary to stay away from everyone and everything drug related. We have reservations about this, never again going around certain people and places. Leaving options open seems to be necessary. These options can de detrimental.

Relationships are among the top reasons for relapse. During active addiction, there is much dysfunction. Many times there has been a tremendous amount of damage between two people. Imagine the damage if both parties are addicts. Sometimes the damage is done and can't be undone, and the relationship becomes irreconcilable. Too much water under the bridge makes recovery more of a struggle. Sometimes the only option is to stay away. Cut your losses!

We always have healthy options. Doing the right thing and making good honest choices may be hard in the beginning, but it gets easier as time passes. There is a method of study called me-ology that teaches admit your wrongs, forgive yourself and move forward. Me-ology is a study of your own integrity, doing the right thing for yourself and others. An example: If you are walking along and the person ahead of you drops a $10 bill, you have the option of picking it up and pocketing it or calling to the person and telling him he just dropped his money. You may justify pocketing the money because you are broke, but what is the best choice for you? Is your integrity only worth $10? Fact is the monetary amount shouldn't matter; you can't place a value on integrity. It feels good to do the right thing. We are worthy of doing what is right and good.

Changing everything and going into unfamiliar avenues of life is overwhelming and takes courage. Sadly our behavior will always look for options to take the easy way out. We must stand fast!

The story of Abraham in Romans 4 says God promised Abraham a son he desperately wanted. God sent Abraham to a wilderness that was unfamiliar, a place he had never been, with only the faith that God would stand on his promise. With no reservations, Abraham chose to give up all he knew and just go. His courage and faith paid off with not only a son, but because of his obedience Abraham became the "father of many nations."

Recovery can make a multitude of changes in our lives. We must make good choices and forego those options that can derail us.

OUR STORIES ARE NOT NEW

Sampson was the strongest man anyone knew. He was praised for his physical strength. But like ordinary men, he had his weakness. Sampson had an obsession with women. He realized this, yet would test himself. His arrogance told him he could resist anything. On this particular walk down the street where the prostitutes lived, Sampson met his demise. He met Delilah, gave into temptation and acted on his desires.

In recovery we are much like Sampson. We know certain people, places and things should be avoided. We become full of pride and arrogant in our success and feel we are on the other side of recovery. We feel like we've worked through our addiction and can handle anything.

Knowing it can be destructive to our well being, we test our strength. We flirt with temptation. Before we realize it, we're caught up in "using" again.

We know what happened to Sampson. Ashamed and guilt ridden, he met an untimely death. He just couldn't resist temptation.

Don't let this happen to you. Resist temptation! It's a lot smarter to resist than to test yourself.

OUT OF SIGHT, OUT OF MIND

At some point we are probably going to find ourselves in jail or in an institution. Then we find ourselves surrounded by people with the same problem; we have a connection. We have acquaintances and make friends. But in trying to cope with our circumstances, we realize we are lonely without family.

We feel it's necessary to hear from loved ones. They owe us that! When it doesn't happen as often as we think it should, we go through a series of emotions – feelings of abandonment, rejection, insecurity, discouragement, fear and anger. The most dangerous of these is anger. This anger creates resentment. Soon we realize we're all alone with hate in our hearts.

So far, all this is about us. Addiction itself is selfish. We need for everyone to go along with our agenda, to do and act accordingly. We become very needy and continue to be even though there has been an intervention. Remember, if there is no change, nothing changes.

At some point we have to begin thinking of others. Take a look at the pain and chaos we've caused in their lives. Realize the control and manipulation we imposed on the people we love. Duh! How could we do this things to people we claim to love? Yet we still somehow think we deserve more respect than we're being shown.

I was once asked, "Just how significant do you think you are? What have you done in others' lives? Have you made a positive difference for them?

How much are we really missed? It's possible we caused so much devastation no one wants to even think about us.

I asked my wife, mom and a friend whose son was in rehab what they thought when we were out of circulation. Moni, my wife, said it was a break. She knew I was safe. She didn't have to be responsible for me or what I was doing and didn't have to worry about something being wrong when the phone rang. While I was away, she had time to work things out in her head. About writing or communication? She said by the end of the day, after taking care of the daily routine, assuming all the responsibilities for both of us, working, taking care of home, vehicles, meals, laundry and the children, she was exhausted. She was too tired to write – period! She, also, said somedays I should have counted it as a blessing I didn't hear from her. It would not have been warm, fuzzy and supportive. Okay! I know where she stands as far as my old behavior is concerned.

My mom said she could finally breathe. But I wasn't out of mind; she still worried about my return home. If she didn't think about me or count the days on the calendar until I would be home, she didn't worry. She knew I was safe. Each time in rehab she had a sense of relief and thanked God that one day this would be over. Yet she lived in fear that I still wouldn't get it (change).

My friend said it was such a relief to stop trying to keep everything quiet. She didn't have to continuously make excuses and cover-up for her son. She didn't have to keep saying she was sorry for what she thought was her fault. She said, "I didn't have to fix what was not my problem." She was tired and angry and didn't really want to write and say things she would regret later. There was already going to be enough pain to work through.

This lesson was very difficult for me to write. There was a tremendous amount of pain rekindled in the hearts and minds of the people I love. I now care how they feel. They cared enough to relive those painful days.

It was hard for them to relate those "out of sight, out of mind" feelings. It was equally hard to hear them. Our prayer should be for

God to let them see it in their hearts to let us back into their lives. And we should thank God every day when they do.

Our responsibility is to change – to make such a definite change that everyone says, "Wow!"

"For you know when your faith is tested, your endurance has a chance to grow. So let it grow, for when your endurance is fully developed, you will be perfect and complete, needing nothing" (James 1:3-4).

PAIN – RESENTMENT – FORGIVENESS

The beginning of addiction can often be attributed to mental or emotional pain. Drugs made me feel better about myself. The pain stemming from I'm not good enough, I'm not as good as so and so, Mom or Dad hates me, they didn't want me, they treat me differently or whatever the situation causes low self-esteem and resentment.

This is or was our perception of what happened. I could be too sensitive to situations and certainly too emotional. The drugs dulled my emotions and took away my pain. At first it was relief from pain; then the drugs gave me courage and finally a sense of security. I thought I felt normal for a change.

Then I began to feel so good about myself, I'm almost courageous. I blame everyone else for my insecurities. Everyone else has a problem, not me. Along the way, I'm damaging relationships because my resentments have turned to anger. I'm progressing to the point of arrogance. I'm stepping on the hearts of loved ones and beginning to do to others what I perceive was done to me. I'm spreading my pain to every relationship I have.

I think I can beat the system, but the consequences of my actions are catching up with me. I'm feeling more pain. The drugs have begun to work against me. Nothing is as lovely as before. Instead of sunshine, I always see clouds. I can't look in the mirror for fear of seeing myself. My motivation is gone. My demeanor and physical appearance are deteriorating.

I am ashamed, but this still can't be my fault. I know the things I have done were wrong, but I wouldn't have done them if so and so hadn't happened. How could my life have become so miserable? Everyone thinks it's my own fault. Whatever!

Forget about fault and think about responsibility. It is my responsibility to recover. The first step to recovery is to forgive the pain with which we started. "You can pray for anything, and if you believe, you will have it. But when you are praying, first forgive anyone you have anything against, so that your Father in heaven will forgive your sins, too" (Mark 11:24-25).

We ask everyone we have hurt to forgive us. We do that so our hearts can heal. To get forgiveness from others, ask God what can I do today. Do those things and relationships will be reconciled. People will recognize the changes in your life; they will be drawn to you and back into your life.

PANIC

We've come to the end of the road; we ask for help. Then suddenly we realize we'll never be able to "use" again, and we panic. When our stress levels and emotions are too high to have clear conscious thoughts or make clear deliberate decisions, we panic. At times panic is almost uncontrollable and is a natural response, especially in emergencies. For example, when we stumble and know we're past the point of stopping the fall, we lose the ability to think logically. An electrical response is sent to our nervous system which causes an adrenaline rush and maybe sweat.

You would think panic is all mental, in your mind. It's not, panic is physical, too. It's the body reacting to whatever you are experiencing. It begins with fear which signals the adrenaline gland which then releases adrenaline and natural steroids. Blood pressure and heart rate go up, digestion stops, muscle tone changes and pupils dilate. We have a body rush.

Addiction is a learned behavior; we use an unconventional and dangerous method to change the way we feel. We may not be "using" at the moment, but until we are far enough along in recovery, we still have addictive behaviors. We may have subconsciously learned to recreate the sensation we feel when "using." We have the need to feel different, so we create panic, chaos and circumstances for dysfunction.

When not getting what we want, we get agitated and cause people to get defensive and even lose their composure. They react just as we had planned. The chaos accelerates; our breathing becomes erratic; we begin shallow panting and then hyperventilating to the point of dizziness. When we hyperventilate, the carbon dioxide level in the blood stream lowers and makes us lightheaded.

Do we intentionally use this behavior to change the way we feel? Have we learned a familiar behavior where we can get the same mental and physical euphoric feelings that are comparable to "using" and getting a rush?

Some of us may not realize this is what's happening. Now we've been called on it, and it has to stop. Recognize the warnings signs and triggers, whether it's crowds, traffic, arguments, etc. Notice your breathing, slow down, control it and walk away if possible.

Get your mind and body organized. Have a logical plan. Make the steps small; the goal should be achievable. First, access the situation. Secondly, make a plan. Because reason and emotion are completely opposites, organizing makes you think rationally.

Anytime we take purposeful action, we suppress our bad behavior. We get the same effect on our lives and behavior when we pray to God and repent for our sins. Repentance means to completely turn away from our old self and do something different.

"Therefore if anyone is in Christ, there is a new creation; old things have passed away; new things have come. A new life has begun" (2 Corinthians 5:17).

PATIENCE

Patience endures through hardships, overcomes adversity and tolerates every circumstance.

Patience is loving, kind, caring and unselfish.

Patience is humble, never arrogant.

Patience is passive, not aggressive.

Patience is careful to listen and slow to speak.

Patience gives thought to every question and answer, therefore gives good advice.

A person with patience has a pleasant, unhurried demeanor or disposition.

Patience is anxious for nothing.

Patience is still, always listening to that quiet voice inside.

Patience is a virtue given to us so we can better enjoy life.

Patience, at times, is tough to practice. Most of us want what we want; we want it right now, our way and by our own rules.

Galatians 5:22 explains how to go about getting what we really need. "When the Holy Spirit controls our lives, He will produce this kind of fruit in us: love, joy, peace, patience, kindness, goodness, faithfulness, gentleness and self control." The Bible always refers to the "fruit of the spirit," not fruits. Fruit is a package deal.

Patience, also, says slow down, be still and wait. Avoid chaos!

Slow down! We live in a rapidly changing society. Many times we rush to keep up or get ahead and stay ahead. When we stop thinking things through, we miss detail; our plans become incomplete.

Be still! We need to calm down and be quiet long enough to take instructions. We might hear something important. We need to be still and calm to enjoy our families and friends.

Wait! We need to wait for our feelings to change and wait until we can better control our emotions. Wait before we act; waiting can change outcomes.

Most of all wait on God's timing and God's plan. Good things come to those who wait. "Those who are patient and wait on the Lord will find new strength. They will fly high on wings like eagles. They will run and not grow weary. They will walk and not faint" (Isaiah 40:31).

PEACE OF MIND

How and from where does peace of mind come? When all the drugs are gone, so is our suspicious thinking. We must give up our resentments. Holding onto grudges takes away happiness and joy we need for recovery. We have to stop letting past failures preoccupy our minds. Worrying about past mistakes and failures cannot dictate our future unless we allow them to. We should look at these mistakes and failures as growth. We need to live in the present and live for the future. Faith is ours to keep and sustain us in the present; hope is where we see ourselves in the future.

Don't waste time and energy fighting things we cannot change. God give me the serenity to accept the things I cannot change. There is little we can do to change those around us. So stop trying! It's a big enough job changing ourselves.

We have to deal with life on life's terms instead of running away from it. In the past we killed the pain the only way we knew how. Now we have to find constructive ways to deal with pain. When we find life too stressful, we should get out and find good healthy people and build new relationships. Playing the pity party and trying to beat these feelings alone are both recipes for disaster.

We should stop expecting too much of ourselves when the gap between expectations and our abilities are too great. We become unhappy and let down when we don't achieve goals quickly. We may need to lower the demands we are placing on ourselves until we can handle more pressure or until our performance can improve. There's nothing wrong with that!

We need to cultivate virtues of love, honor, loyalty and church attendance. These virtues will give us the peace of mind we seek.

PERFECTIONISM

There are two different perspective ways to look at perfectionism. Psychologically, perfectionism has several facets of behavior as well. Many of us think we have to get this thing called recovery not just right but perfect. We meet and know people in recovery who seem to have it all together; they know all the right things to say and do. They give off an air of perfection. There is no such thing as perfection in recovery. If we don't recognize this fact, we begin to second guess ourselves.

We already see things not as how they are but as how they should be. We set unrealistic goals for ourselves; these goals usually ensure failure which often times causes us to give up or quit altogether. There is no joy or sense of accomplishment until the end of a task. Joy in the journey is often overlooked. If you strive for perfection and think you have to get everything right in recovery, recovery in itself will be miserable.

Perfectionists always believe they have to be the best at what they do. To do our best is not good enough. Because of our pasts and our failures, we try to make no mistakes. We try extremely hard to fit in. Many times we are performing for the benefit of others. We often get ahead of ourselves. Someone may call our hand on our selfishness when we start thinking it's all about us.

After we stumble, we want to give up and quit. We feel like we've failed; we didn't perform well enough; we weren't perfect. Our performance dictates our worth. Since our progress fluctuates from day to day, so does our self-worth.

Spiritually, perfectionism is destructive when we become holier than thou. Recovering addicts who are perfectionists think they should be omniscient (all knowing), omnipotent (all powerful) and omnipresent (everywhere at once). We think we are the only ones who can do it all and do it right. When our performance isn't up to par, our subconscious is there reminding us of the drugs that helped in the past. We can't listen to this subconscious; drugs are what put us here.

We have to stop beating ourselves up for our lapses and failures. To dwell on them only causes discouragement which leads to depression. The idea is to make progress; perfection is not attainable on this side of heaven. Only God knows all and can do all. We actually know very little and can only do our best. When we fall, we need to get up and try again. We must plan and strive for a brighter and healthier tomorrow. God accepts us the way we are; we have to learn to accept ourselves.

What should we do now?

- Be responsible and patient. In the beginning it's hard to comprehend all we need to know. We've always wanted to get what we want when we want it. True recovery doesn't work that way.

- Start thinking in terms of black and white, right and wrong. Manipulators, co-dependents and enablers think in grey areas only. Perfectionists need to realize their way may not be the only right way.

- Set realistic and attainable goals. In the beginning we do baby steps, one day at a time. We accept "good enough" and "just for today" and move on to the next task. Learn from mistakes; everybody makes them.

- Be humble. Try your best to keep pride from being a hindrance. Accept good advice and suggestions.

- Face reality. Face life as it is; don't dwell on how it could or should be. Change should come slowly; otherwise life will be overwhelming or we'll leave out vital steps in our recovery.

- Be accountable. Acknowledging our imperfections helps to release us from our pride that says we have to be perfect.

If we want to be successful in recovery, we must find joy in our journey. We will never be flawless or infallible, so we can stop trying. It normally takes most of our lives to reach a level of maturity that reflects wisdom. Each step we take in that direction of maturity pleases God and is another step farther away from our past.

Perfectionists and recovering addicts need to find their self worth not in their performances but in knowing they are God's children, his creations. We are perfect in his sight but imperfect in our behavior.

Knowing the psychological and theological aspects of perfectionism is only a minute piece of knowledge valuable to our recovery. Confronting our bad behavior and cultivating our knowledge and love of Jesus Christ will exhibit growth in us. So what does it mean for believers that Christ's sacrifice perfected forever those who are being sanctified? We are being made perfect and holy progressively through our walk with Him, even though we have a long way to go. As we let God work in us, He protects us.

"I don't mean to say that I have already achieved these things or that I have already reached perfection. But I keep working toward that day when I will finally be all that Christ has saved me for and wants me to be. No dear brothers and sisters, I am not all I should be, but I am focusing all my energies on this one thing. Forgetting the past and looking forward to what lies ahead, I strain to reach the end of the race and receive the prize for which God, through Jesus Christ, is calling us up to heaven" (Philippians 3:12-14).

PERFORMANCE

Some of us perform for the sole reason of gaining approval from someone or people in general. We have a need to be needed. The first memory that comes to mind as to why I became performance oriented is my mom teaching me to be a leader. She would say, "Why would you follow when you could lead?"

Some have the natural ability to lead; some of us are influenced. There is nothing wrong with taking charge unless it becomes a control issue or until we begin to get our self-worth from our performance or how we perceive our performance for those we were trying to impress.

Leadership requires continuously putting yourself out front, constantly being the center of attention and opening yourself up for criticism. Leading requires discipline in organization and, also, requires answering questions and giving advice. An intelligent leader delegates tasks and doesn't make himself responsible for doing the entire job.

Our performance driven behavior tries to do it all for the praise we need in order to change the way we feel. We often get so caught up in performing we lose sight of leading. Leadership is either successful or ends in failure. Addicts, being very sensitive, take failures to heart. Our self-esteem takes a hit. Yet we don't learn.

In order to lead or remain in control, we become people pleasers. Without thinking, we volunteer for so much we begin to feel used, especially if we realize we were manipulated into taking on a project.

It's worse when others don't express what we feel is the appropriate gratitude.

The truth is we have put a burden on ourselves. Our intentions were to serve people; in return we would feel good about ourselves. But when we give and give and give, we lose sight of self until there is nothing left to give. Then we discover drugs. The drugs give us a sense of well being. They give us energy and make us feel better about ourselves. Here we go again! Drugs are just what I needed to perform even better than before.

The drugs work for awhile, but soon we have to use more or add another one to perform to the extremes we feel are necessary. Then the drugs stop working and actually are working against us. We don't want to be the leader anymore. We become tired of performing and just want to be left alone. After being the center of attention for so long, it's extremely hard to isolate ourselves from family and friends who are expecting us to get things done.

While in active addiction we do some performances we are ashamed of the next morning. I would like to say that's not us, that was the addiction. Sadly enough, it was us. Having a performance driven behavior and under the influence of drugs give us the courage to do things we normally would not do.

When in recovery we need help, but before we know it, our performances are giving the people what they want to hear. We are in recovery for everyone but ourselves. We can perform everyone's program except ours. We can recite the steps, use cool sounding terminology and even know some appropriate scriptures. Performance! We perform to feel good but don't necessarily feel good about ourselves.

We tend to think the same about our behavior before God; we need to perform. God does call on us to give our best as far as our talents and gifts, but we think more in terms of what people expect. If we are good ole boys and girls, do good things for people, show respect, get involved in church, drive the church bus, do prison ministry and perform other such duties, we will "work" our way into heaven.

1 Corinthians 9:24-27 tells us, "Remember that in a race everyone

runs, but only one person gets the prize. You must, also, run in such a way that you will win. All athletes practice self control. They do it to win a prize that will fade away, but we do it for an eternal prize. So I run straight to the goal with a purpose in every step. I am not like a boxer who misses his punches. I discipline my body like an athlete, training it to do what it should. Otherwise, I fear that after preaching to others, I myself might be disqualified."

THE PIT

Have you ever been betrayed by someone close to you, someone on whom you rely or someone you consider a best friend? Have you every betrayed anyone? This exercise is not meant to rekindle old resentments or guilt. It is an attempt to open our minds and reevaluate the choice of friends with which we wish to associate.

In addiction we are confused along several lines. Why do we form relationships with people who have unhealthy habits and no morals? We are lead to those who possess the same behavior we have. We choose people who are like us. These include "using" pals, dealers, liars, cheaters, thieves, scam artists and people who use and hurt others. We become caught up in our secrets, the discrete privacy between parties and the camaraderie in our circles.

We have shared the euphoria while "using;" we have shared the intensity of the high with these folks. They were there over and over again when we got our relief and felt the best we had ever felt. All this draws us closer, and we begin to think we love this person or group of people. We think these are the ones on whom we can rely. We turn our backs on our family and real friends, thinking they have never done anything so great for us.

Normally about the third stage of addiction when the drugs have begun to work against us, our behavior gets noticeable; our world starts crumbling down around us. People get suspicious of us or some member of our network. Someone gets questioned or caught; he gets scared. His next move is to divert the attention elsewhere, and the betrayal begins. Haven't you heard "there's no honor among thieves?"

Another reason people betray others is jealousy. We all have come in contact with someone who seems to always be favored, who can get out of any problem, who always comes out smelling like a rose. This could be you until one of your so called friends throws you under the bus.

Then there is the honor system, but we leave our options open. We never give up our best connection until he betrays us. Then there of those of us who need acceptance to the point we'll take responsibility for everyone. When the smoke clears, we realize they betrayed us for letting that happen. Most of us are good people with kind, caring hearts, but to be accountable for others and their drug behavior is just plain stupid.

Drugs have a way of stopping our mental and emotional growth. We have the inability to accept responsibility for our own actions. We're just like children – I didn't do it, it's not my fault, he did it, too!

Our addictive behavior won't allow us to be accountable for our wrongs. We try to defer the attention on to someone else in an effort to cover up and stop anyone from seeing who and what we have become. We are so ashamed of our own behavior, we'll try anything to make ourselves look and feel better. Betrayal is another example of adding more guilt to what we already have.

In Genesis 37, Joseph, one of the twelve sons of Jacob, was the favorite. His brothers felt betrayed and had so much resentment and jealousy they disrobed Joseph in hopes of exposing his imperfections. They threw him into a pit. In our clouded minds, we can feel animosity towards someone and even hatred because of our jealousy or for being betrayed by him. If we are like Joseph and have nothing of which to be ashamed, if our hearts are pure and our behavior is in line with God, we don't have to worry how deep the pit is or how dark it gets.

In the darkness, as the story goes, if we are righteous, we have the comfort to know God always sends a savior. Some of us have a misconceived notion that God has betrayed us by putting us in the pit. We're like Joseph. The dark places are part of the process of getting where we need to be to fulfill His purpose.

PROGRESS, NOT PERFECTION

Why do we expect perfection and can not just accept progress?

Many times when we have begun our journey to recovery, our health improves and we have a tendency to forget where our lives were in the very recent past. Our behavior was and is unacceptable because we have stopped any and all mental and emotional growth with the use of drugs. We have developed many character defects simply because of our self-centeredness and our addiction. We have submitted our lives to complete dysfunction.

We may neglect to "stay in the problem" which is "I and my behavior." Instead we want to point out the shortcomings of everyone else. We are quick to recognize anything anyone says or does that makes them less than perfect; this makes us feel better about ourselves.

Some of us can conform to a program quite easily. In a structured situation, we can follow the rules and be seemingly intelligent. Most probably we will be labeled a leader. Since our behavior has not changed, we still have enough arrogance that tells us we are in control. With a new title comes attitude; this attitude makes us feel superior. Then we become overbearing and conduct ourselves as if we know it all and have perfected this thing called recovery.

Our behavior did not get to this point in one day; the progression was slow. Therefore we should expect progress to come slowly in recovery. Many people have an idea, when they feel better physically and learn a few terms and inspirational Bible verses, they have a handle on recovery.

None of us have progressed from where we were to anywhere near perfection. Recovery is a process that will develop our behavior to a higher and better, more advanced standard of living. Recovery is not a cut and dry curriculum. Just having the knowledge does not change us instantly. Recovery does not come from what we learned in the past but from what we seek in the future.

The problem with understanding the concept too quickly or "getting it" immediately is that this is how we've always operated. Whatever it is we want, we want it right now. There is no lasting gratification and success; easy come, easy go. The point is we should take recovery in steps, stay connected and continue in recovery. None of us are immune to relapse.

There are people in our lives who put unreasonable expectations on us. They seem to be watching and waiting for us to stumble, to fail so they can say, "I told you so." Understand, this isn't necessarily about us; it could be about them and their failures. If we live up to their expectations and fail, it makes them feel better about themselves.

Of course, there are those whom we have hurt so many times they no longer have any confidence in us. They have simply given up hope of us making progress, much less reaching perfection.

When we give our lives to Christ, we repent and change our lives for the better. When Christians mess up, people think they must not really be Christians. People expect Christians to be perfect. On the same token, we, as addicts, think we have to be perfect before we are worthy of the acceptance and love of Christ. God desires perfection but always accepts progress. He says come to me just as you are.

Matthew 7:1-5 reads,

> Stop judging others, and you will not be judged. For others will treat you as you treat them. Whatever

measure you use in judgment, it will be used to measure how you are judged. And why worry about a speck in your friend's eye when you have a log in yours? How can you think of saying. "Let me help you get rid of that speck in your eye," when you can't see past the log in your eye? Hypocrite! First get rid of the log from your own eye; then perhaps you will see well enough to deal with the speck in your friend's eye.

REALITY

Most addicts live in a fantasy world. Using drugs has clouded our minds. From our very first use, our thinking was altered. We began to see life through rose colored glasses. Our "using" gave us a false sense of truth and reality. Our reasoning was altered; we could rationalize and manipulate with the best.

Those of us who have crossed the line into dependency have some serious reality issues. We constantly and consistently want what we want when we want it; fact is we demand it. We force and manipulate people in every situation.

Our addiction interferes with our ability to conduct ourselves in a reasonable manner. We can not wait on delayed gratification; it must be right now. This causes us to have irrational and unrealistic expectations of others. These same expectations of instant gratification make recovery harder for us.

We have to remember that most things we hold dear materialized slowly. If it's worth having and keeping, we must be ready to accept that it will take time. Recovery is like this. Our addiction did not happen in a day; recovery will not either.

In recovery we, step by step, examine our lives, identify the pain which is the root of our addiction, face this pain and accept that we cannot change it. The only thing we can do is work to a place where we can forgive. When we are examining this pain, we may realize instead of this hurt being purposely directed at us, it's no more than just reality.

The problem may not be what happened but how we processed the event in our minds. Addicts, as a whole, are very sensitive people; we take everything to heart. We take responsibility for anything that goes wrong, thinking we caused it or deserved it. We begin to think we're no good. This thinking may be our own doing, may be caused by someone else or may just be due to circumstances.

Whatever caused the pain should not be our focus. The focus should be on a solution. We are our own solution. The responsibility in recovery is not to focus on what happened or who caused it. It's our responsibility to acknowledge it's our problem and recover from it.

We must be diligent and patient in recovery simply because of the feelings and behaviors developed through our addiction. We have cultivated a dangerous lifestyle of intense behavior. This intense behavior carries over into recovery. Have you ever heard if your behavior doesn't change, nothing changes?

The reason why most of us chose to use drugs was to find peace and comfort. In reality this peace and comfort can only be found within ourselves, without the use of outside stimuli. A life filled with patience, kindness, giving and sharing will be our solution.

Everyone deserves to receive and give love. "Love bears all things, hopes all things, believes all things and endures all things" (1 Corinthians 13:4-7).

Most of us have thoughts and ideas of our futures, visions of how we want our lives to be transformed. These dreams and visions can only be manifested by action. We must put our addictions and bad behaviors in our pasts so recovery can become a reality.

RELAPSE

What happens? Something or nothing happens. Why does it happen? We become happy, sad, lonely, frustrated or bored. What were we thinking? Stinkin' thinkin' such as I can reward myself, I can do just one, I can control it this time or I've "got" this recovery thing. There may be triggers that set us off. Are we impulsive? If you're like me, I act before I think. At this point in my life, that's a lame excuse.

Do triggers and impulses work together? What does it mean to relapse? Addiction means we have a disease. I've always had a problem with the "disease" concept. A disease is something that you can't control. Disease is uncontrollable without intervention. I'll be the first to admit that my addiction is definitely dis – ease.

The Bible says old sinful ways have passed, and we have been created new. What part of me can't get that concept? I do know God has taken that desire from me, so why do I sin? Because I was born in sin; it is my sinful nature. I still have temptations.

Steve says it takes action to sin. It takes the same action to relapse. We look at relapse as a weakness. 2 Corinthians 12:9 says, "For when I am weak, then I am strong."

"Keep watching and praying that you may not enter into temptation; the spirit is willing, but the flesh is weak" (Matthew 26:41). Also, refer to 1 Corinthians 10:13.

Remember the temptations that come into your life are no

different than those other people experience. God is faithful. He will keep the temptation from becoming so strong that you can't stand up to it. When you are tempted, He will show you a way out so you won't give in to temptation. "The Lord knows how to rescue the godly from temptation and to keep the unrighteous under punishment for the day of judgment" 2 Peter 2:9). I encourage you to read all of 2 Peter, Chapter 2.

Avoid people, places and things. In 2 Peter 2:18-19 those who have just escaped wicked living are lured back into sin. They were promised freedom, but they themselves are slaves to sin and corruption. You are a slave to whatever controls you. Verse 20 tells us when people escape the wicked of the world by learning about our Lord and Savior Jesus Christ and then get tangled up in sin again, they are worse off than ever.

To stay on the right track, first of all I avoid places. In doing this, I'm avoiding people and things that are bad for me.

One of the most sure fire ways to avoid relapse is to develop good, strong relationships. We all have a need for relationships. We have a need for emotional connections. These emotional connections are essential to our lives; they're necessary for survival. Most people need other people. That's why we form families, social groups, cultures and even nations. We have evolved to function not alone but together.

We are drawn to people we like, those who share our beliefs and values. We should nurture good relationships. In hazardous situations those bonds with family, friends and Jesus Christ become extremely important to our chances of survival. The more we strengthen those bonds, the better we will be able to face adversity when it comes, and it always will.

"We can rejoice, too, when we run into problems and trials, for we know they are good for us – they help us learn and endure. And endurance develops strength of character in us, and character strengthens our confident expectation of salvation" (Romans 5:3).

RESPONSIBILITY

We have hurts in our past which continue to cause us pain. We have to revisit these hurts, analyze them and see our part in them. Failing to do so only harbors and strengthens resentments already there. We are always told we must forgive. We know that, but forgiving is not that easy. This is a big order! The program says "one day at a time."

Some programs will ask about our history and suggest the most horrendous offense against us caused the pain from which we are desperately trying to escape. To identify and examine the pain is the first and most important entity of recovery. The incident that seems so evident as the cause of our pain may not be the real problem. Yes, it caused the most hurt and rage and the biggest resentment, but, my suggestion is, in most of us, the incident caused a chain of negative thoughts about ourselves. What's wrong with me? Maybe I deserved it. It was so degrading I feel worthless, belittled and undeserving now.

My suggestion is the pain is ultimately in us. We are intelligent, creative and sensitive people with very low self-esteem. Without knowledge of addiction, society in general is not helpful. People tend to categorize addicts as dirty, low-down, no good, sorry, lying, cheating, stealing, non-contributing members of society. We tend to live up to their expectations because our low self-esteem makes us believe it. Low self-esteem will tell us we are not worthy of any better life than we are now living. That's not true! We deserve to be happy and pain free living fulfilled lives.

We are not responsible for what caused us our pain, but it is our responsibility to recover from it. Our responsibility is to recognize (1) we are addicts with a common disease of addiction, (2) addiction was caused by pain and (3) the problem is me.

Next we must accept the fact we can't do recovery alone. We must seek good healthy relationships. We need a good sponsor or accountability partner. The responsibility is on us to take suggestions, study them and use what we can at the time.

When we become anxious about things out of our control, we should use them as an opportunity to grow instead of a reason to run. There are hidden blessings in our challenges and difficulties.

Don't waste time on what might have been or if the situation had been different. Start where we are now. Accept the things we can not change and search for hope. Time clean and time with God, being still and quiet, heals all things.

"My child, don't lose sight of good planning and insight. Hang on to them, for they will fill you with life and bring you honor and respect. They will keep you safe on your way and keep your feet from stumbling" (Proverbs 3:21-23).

SACRIFICE

The definition of sacrifice is to offer something precious, to surrender something for something else, to suffer loss or to give up something. As addicts and alcoholics, most of us have no comprehension of sacrifice. What have we ever sacrificed for the benefit of others? Do we sacrifice our time, money or any other part of our lives? Do we even know how to give of ourselves for any other than selfish reasons?

Addiction itself is a selfish behavior. None of us "used" for the benefit of someone else. It was for self and self alone!

There are some of us who have been labeled "functional" addicts or alcoholics. Maybe we do go to work and pay the bills, attend family functions, go to church from time to time. We present ourselves as productive members of society. Maybe we even do something nice for our neighbors, but we probably expect something in return.

We do these things to look good to the outside world. But what about inside our families? We usually sacrifice nothing. Actually, we expect them to sacrifice for us. If we are involved, our selfishness dictates their every move. Our agendas come first. Family members have to tip-toe around us. They put up with our hangovers. They hold their breaths waiting for our next use. They wait on our return before making plans. They can forget about us being on time for anything.

We rob our families of valuable and constructive family time. We do have a considerable amount of knowledge that our children can use in their growth. We just don't have the time or patience to impart it to them.

Life is all about us! In our addiction we live in the here and now, getting what we want when we want it. We have to be self satisfied. All conditions must be favorable to us.

Then the lucky ones of us who get sober through good healthy recovery programs learn that life is not just about us any longer. With a spiritual foundation and having God in our lives, we begin to behave better and live all-around healthier lives.

We may have unhealthy relationships we have to sacrifice. But is it really a sacrifice if the relationship is unhealthy?

We may have to rearrange our priorities. We are what we are taught. In my growing up, my parents worked and sacrificed their whole lives so we children could have everything we needed and most of what we wanted. Probably what we needed was fewer monetary things and more of their time – time to teach us responsibility.

During my active addiction, I gave to keep everyone off my back so nobody or nothing interfered with my agenda. My wife referred to these as "guilt gifts." I was trying to justify my spending and my not being there.

In recovery we can learn to sacrifice. Some sacrifices will be hard for us. Many will be so meaningful to those who love us. We can stop being selfish and self-centered. We can change the way our story ends.

We all have the potential to change but not under our own power. God wants to change our character and behavior. Change can and will come.

"I plead with you to give your bodies to God. Let them be a living and holy sacrifice – the kind He will accept. When you think of what He has done for you, is this too much to ask? Don't copy the behavior and customs of this world, but let God transform you into a new person by changing the way you think. Then you will know what God wants you to do, and you will know how good and pleasing and perfect His will really is" (Romans 12:1-2).

SANITY

Is being sane the same as being normal? Is sanity clear thinking? Clinically or drug induced? Insanity is a mental health issue; the brain is not structurally sound. Clinically, we would be in a psychiatric hospital. I'm going to have to give you a backwards approach to this topic. I'm still working on this one myself.

There is a debate among professionals. It's the nurture debate; basically it says we are what we are taught. We learn from our parents and peers. Many of us had parents who worked; we were raised by others or we raised ourselves. Many may not have had good role models. Many addicts use their upbringing or lack thereof to justify their addiction.

We're really good at justification. We justify our actions when drugs become our focus. We start making wrong decisions and create this crazy way of thinking. We deny our own hearts. Drug abuse brings on personality change. We begin to rationalize insane ideas.

Men may rationalize that his wife and children deserve his mental and physical abuse. Women may rationalize that it's okay to drop off the children with relatives or friends so they can go buy drugs, do drugs and risk going to jail, hospital or morgue.

Users become so drug induced we manipulate every situation and every relationship in our lives. We actually manipulate ourselves into believing our deceptions and rationalizations. This is insanity.

Insanity for me is thinking I only have myself to live for. It's all about me! "Your children will be like shepherds wandering around in the wilderness forty years. They will pay for your faithlessness" (Numbers 14:33).

So today I don't profess to be totally sane. It's a process of getting better. I'm working on it, asking God to come into my life, live in me everyday and give me peace of mind.

Is learned behavior our excuse? Is our drug abuse our responsibility? Is insanity bad habits? Is sanity normal, clean, sober choices?

When we leave here, is it reasonable or insane to believe everything will be okay? Have our using pals and dealers changed? "Those fake teachers who are so anxious to win your favor are not doing it for your good. They are trying to shut you off from me, so that you will pay more attention to them" (Galatians 4:17).

NA says we didn't become this way overnight, so easy does it. We should give ourselves time to recover.

SECURITY

What do we need in recovery? It's necessary to have a sense of security. In our study of addiction, we found we have some sort of mental or emotional pain inside us. Then we discovered what we thought was a solution for our pain and problems. Alcohol and drugs became our comfort zone.

Problem is we have used for so long, the alcohol and drugs were controlling us. Our lives either stood still or regressed; they definitely didn't progress. But in our many attempts to stop, we feared the unknown and returned to the familiar – alcohol and drugs. No matter how wrong or dysfunctional, familiarity is comfortable.

In active addiction we lose many opportunities including jobs, material wealth and relationships. We can normally tolerate the loss of employment because we can find another job. Material wealth can be replaced, but losing our spouse, children or families can be critical to recovery. If we have affirmation that loved ones will wait for us, we have hope. If we have their assurance, we have security.

Everyone needs love and compassion. Companionship gives us a sense of completion. When we feel our self-worth is validated by another person and we are rejected by this person, there is a void. We make bad decisions to fill this void. Perhaps we should first take a good long hard look at the void. This person could have been a wrong choice from the very beginning. I have a friend who tells this part of his recovery: "I am holding on to her as if I have nothing else. I think maybe, when I can let her go, God will have someone better for me."

Holding on to a relationship just because it's familiar and comfortable can be dysfunctional and destructive. Nevertheless, we feel like our happiness depends on this relationship. The truth is we must first be content with ourselves; we cannot depend on others for our happiness. When we can be content with ourselves, we will have a sense of security.

How can we be content with ourselves? There's not a quick fix. We have to be quiet and wait on God's timing. We have to practice patience, kindness and sensitivity to others. From God we find security.

"We can rejoice, too, when we run into problems and trials, for we know they are good for us. They help us learn to endure. And endurance develops strength of character in us, and character strengthens our confident expectations of salvation (strengthens hope). And this expectation of hope will not disappoint us" (Romans 5:3-5).

SELF CONTROL

Instead of practicing self control, it's easier to use excuses for our behavior. These excuses range from I'm an addict to if they think I'm using, I might as well because recovery is too hard.

What is self control? Most of us think self-control is having will power. Will power is gritting your teeth, white knuckling trying to hold on and reciting, "Just say no." Relying just on our will power usually results in failure.

Self control doesn't come naturally. Our nature is to do wrong or to do what comes the easiest. Practicing self control is hard. Without self control our desires become obsessions; our will power is just not strong enough to hold on; we give in and use. One is too many and a thousand is not enough; the cravings take over.

So how do we develop self control? First we have to stay clean and think clearly. We must make a decision to turn our will and our lives over to the care of God. Self control then comes to us as a gift from God. My dad says, "Where else would I get self control but from God?"

Self control is one of the fruits of the spirit. Much like the fruit on a tree which has to grow and ripen, self control, also, has to grow and mature. As we mature in self control, we begin to have patience and endurance. These produce godliness; godliness leads to love and the love of all people.

When we realize we have developed some self control, we then realize what self control means to us. It means having discipline, having boundaries, having standards of trust and integrity in our lives. We have control of our thoughts, our tongues and our actions.

I Peter 1:13-16 reads,

> So think clearly and exercise self control. Look forward to the special blessings that will come to you at the return of Jesus Christ. Obey God because you are his children. Don't slip back into your old ways of doing evil; you didn't know any better then. But now you must be holy in everything you do, just as God, who chose you to be his children, is holy. For He himself has said, "You must be holy because I am holy."

Holy is a word that is often misinterpreted. Holy doesn't mean being perfect or righteous; it means to be set apart from others.

Our self control grows the closer we grow to God. God gives us his own character one step at a time, one day at a time. With God's character, we are set apart.

Galatians 5:16-17 says,

> So I advise you to live according to your new life in the Holy Spirit. Then you won't be doing what your sinful nature craves. The old sinful nature loves to do evil; which is just the opposite from what the Holy Spirit wants. And the Spirit gives us desires opposite from what the sinful nature desires. These two forces are constantly fighting each other, and your choices are never free from this conflict.

Galatians 5:22-23 says,

> But when the Holy Spirit controls our lives, He will produce this kind of fruit in us: love, joy, peace, patience, kindness, goodness, faithfulness, gentleness and self control. Here there is no conflict with the law.

SENSITIVE PEOPLE

It's been said that 90% of alcoholics and drug addicts are very sensitive people. Haven't you heard of the "good ole drunk" who has a big heart but just drinks too much? Most of us have a tendency to cry at the drop of a hat or at least get emotional over the most insignificant thing. I need a box of tissue just to watch "Little House on the Prairie."

I can remember as a young child seeing people upset and crying. I felt badly for them; I actually hurt for them. I didn't like hurting and would distance myself. I'd go climb a tree, play ball or just think of something else if I couldn't get away.

I remember my parents didn't get along very well. Many times the next night after they argued, my dad would come home after drinking and say things so out of character for him. His behavior would frighten me. I soon recognized alcohol was the cause for this behavior. My dad was and is a very sensitive person with a kind heart and demeanor. He would never have said anything to hurt anyone if he had not been drinking.

It turns out that maybe I did have the predisposition to be an addict. I have the same sensitive personality that discovered drugs to be the solution for the way I felt when I was sad, mad, upset or afraid. Addiction could, also, be the result of learned behavior. Either way, now as I look back and can think clearly about my past, I know that drugs were the wrong choice for my discomfort. It turns out that our solution for pain ultimately hurts us and others.

There have been times when we've been hurt or challenged. Being sensitive, we don't have it in us to return the treatment. Alcohol or drugs may give us "courage" to do so, but it is inevitable that what we say or do while under the influence will be uncharacteristic of who we really are. Being sensitive, caring people, we don't want to cause any undue pain.

Now there is a word – caring. Does this word have a direct correlation to sensitive? Being sensitive means (1)easily hurt or damaged, (2)delicately aware of attitudes and feelings of self and others and (3)capable of indicating minute changes or differences.

Being sensitive, caring people, we want to take care of whomever is hurting. We want to ease their pain. When it's us hurting, we choose the wrong solution. We use the only method we think works for us; it's not a healthy choice. In the attempt to repeatedly kill our pain with chemicals, we create more pain. Eventually we kill any and all emotions to the point where we feel nothing. Feelings and emotions are essential to a person's mental and physical health.

Some of us used to avoid feelings; some used to avoid showing emotions. Using led to more pain and then paranoia. Our kind and caring natures became angry and resentful. The solution we sought for our pain ended up causing us more pain.

When we first get clean and everything starts to come together, we start to remember the times when the drugs "worked." We forget about our selfishness and how we've hurt others. This is dangerous thinking! We have to stay clean long enough to remember and accept the bad times. We have to continually see the big picture.

My prayer for today and the remainder of my life is I ask God to be with me and correct my selfish nature and to not let me hurt anyone today. I want to be sensitive to others' needs before my own. It is my desire to be a godly man and exhibit the joy that has been shown to me through the love and grace of Christ Jesus. I am thankful I know Christ. Joy comes from serving Jesus, caring for others and knowing that He will take care of me when I put myself last. I thank God He was so sensitive to the world's needs that He sent His only son to die for me and all of mankind. And everybody says, "Amen."

SIN ON THIS SIDE

We as a society and a great number of Christians have a diluted idea of sin. What is sin? Are some sins worse than others? Are some sins socially accepted?

My ministry and testimony are about drug addiction and recovery. Many people who do not understand having a drug problem or chemical dependency think addiction is a weakness. It's not. It is a desperate attempt to take away some kind of mental or emotional pain. Drug addiction is sort of like self medication, a cure for what hurts.

Addiction is a sin. Addicts hurt themselves and others. Addicts should be judged as sinners. But these same judges should look at their own lives before passing judgment on others.

In the Bible, sin is sin; one sin is just as bad as another. In today's society, some sins have more or less become socially acceptable. Just look at homosexuality, social drinking and legalized gambling. Why is homosexuality accepted but prostitution isn't? Why is addiction to pain medication prescribed by a doctor more socially accepted than smoking crack? Which is worse: the person who sells his/her body to buy drugs or the person who judges this person? We are not talking about legal issues.

When we see someone in need and turn our backs, we are sinning. In the Bible the Samarian woman who hemorrhaged for twelve years was made to feel ashamed, guilty and dirty by Christians. These

Christians tried to keep her from reaching Jesus. When we know something is wrong or someone is in need and do nothing to help, we are committing sin. It's the sin of omission. Most people are guilty of the sin of omission. Their attitude is if it doesn't affect them, why should they care. It's sin when we know we should love as Jesus did and don't.

Granted, some sins are more offensive than others. Actually some things have become so socially accepted they're not even considered sins. We tend to justify and excuse anything that doesn't hurt someone. This is wrong. The Bible says, "The wages of sin is death" (Romans 6:23).

We addicts know we are sinners. Society judges us. But who will be our ultimate judge? God will not only judge us but those who judged us.

SITUATIONS

We are always faced with situations; we find ourselves in the middle, having to make choices. We often find ourselves in a predicament, searching for the right solution.

Are we grounded in the right place? Do we have a firm foundation on which to stand? Do we make good decisions? Do we make decisions with everyone involved in mind? Are our decisions made selflessly? Most of us make the choice of what's best for ourselves.

Many times we get involved in situations that are none of our business. We have lived and thrived on chaos so long that we just jump right in with our two cents. We should first honestly evaluate the situation and decide if our involvement is even necessary.

We are so sensitive to negativity that any negative reaction to us is regarded as a personal attack. Or we feel like everything that goes wrong is our fault. Everything that goes bad happens to us. Our first thought is the situation must be bad, and there's a personal attack on us.

Satan is on one side of every situation and God is on the other. To whom do we listen? At some point we have to take a stand, to take a position in life and do the right thing. Knowing right from wrong, we should first listen to our hearts. Secondly, we should exercise some patience and be still before acting. Being grounded with God's principles and reflecting his character, our actions will reflect where our hearts really are.

Whether the situations are critical or just some kind of drama, we must realize our part and decide if we have the ability to handle it on our own.

During this year's church softball season, my son DJ was injured in a game. He had a serious knee injury that incapacitated him for a couple of weeks. While disable, in pain and worrying about school and work, DJ began to question why God would do this to him or let this happen to him. I was at a loss in knowing how to respond. I told DJ I know God loves us and does not punish us.

Helpless in knowing more to say, I called a friend. Jimmy F. was a fellow ball player and a minister who has great knowledge and understanding of how to express God's love for us. His easy disposition and great discernment, also, help with his ability to relate God's message. He reminded us of a series of sermons we had heard lately; the topic of these was "if I was the devil, what would I do?"

DJ has a passion for sports and Satan knows it. Doing his job, Satan proceeded to take ball away from DJ for a time. In the midst of his anger, DJ blamed God. He couldn't understand why after he had been doing so well, going to church, inviting people, using softball as a ministry and witnessing God would do this to him.

In any situation we have ourselves, God and Satan. Satan wants us to think God did it. Maybe God does allow Satan to test the faith we have in Jesus Christ.

My dilemma was as in the story where Jesus is at the house in Capernaum. The paraplegic man was carried to the house and lowered through the roof to Jesus where he could be blessed. I felt crippled and inadequate to the point where I needed a friend on whom I could depend. I needed a godly man, one who knew God well who could get DJ where he needed to be, right back into the hands of Jesus.

If we are grounded and if we have faith in God and as Christians practice his principles, we will make good choices. Satan will always tempt us. He tried tempting Jesus, but Jesus stood on solid ground and never faltered.

The moral of this story is, when in the midst of any situation you feel crippled or inadequate, don't hesitate to call for help. We can depend on healthy people for advice and use their ability to see other ways to get past our problems.

SPIRITUAL AWAKENING

Spiritual is intellectual, divine, pure, not material, non secular; it is mental. Awakening is to be aroused from a state, sleep or inaction; it is to be stirred up. An experience is a personal trial, knowledge gained by trial or observation or knowledge gained from suffering or enjoyment; it can be the suffering or enjoyment itself.

At some point in our lives, we have had a spiritual experience. Some recognize it; some don't. There could have been an accident that should have taken our lives. We either recognize God was there and spared us or take it for granted and call it luck.

We wake up from a black out and never consider "why." We are compelled to keep trying to fill that empty hole the quickest and easiest way we can. At some point we have to realize God wants to intervene.

What is a spiritual awakening? A spiritual awakening comes slowly. There is a part of us that wants God and the other part that is our nature, the nature that was created in sin. Most of us have had someone in our lives who tried to witness to us and tell us how great God is. We hear stories about spiritual experiences and how great the feeling is when Jesus comes into our lives.

I wonder what is that feeling I keep hearing about. I know I've asked Jesus to come into my heart, and yet I haven't felt anything but the same old hurt I've always felt.

Why doesn't God's miracle happen to me? Why am I not worthy of God's love? I guess I've been such a bad person and hurt so many people I have to accept the bed I've made for myself.

When I thought my life was over, I decided I would go look for God. I still didn't find him; I had the wrong ideas about what God could do for me. I thought He could just snap his finger and fix everything. I thought I could just mention God and those around me would know I had been healed.

We have to hear the word of God, believe the word of God and participate in our salvation. That's how we'll have a spiritual awakening. It's not always easy. God does make us a promise: "But first seek His kingdom and His righteousness, and all else will be added to you" (Matthew 6:33).

STAYING CONNECTED

When addicts realize they have a problem, first they rely on their own will power. By this time, addiction has taken a toll on us and many others. We don't have the fortitude to make it on our own. We must seek support in recovery.

In recovery there will be times we run into trouble. We will face temptations. We need someone to talk to. If we don't surround ourselves with good healthy relationships, we won't have anyone to turn to in our time of need. We can't afford to let ourselves become bored. Get up and do something for someone in need.

We can't afford to become complacent. We must become diligent in our recovery. Just as we wouldn't let a rattlesnake loose in our house, neither should we succumb to bad habits, laziness and poor judgment. In both cases, we'll end up getting bitten.

Our own will power is not enough. Addiction is bigger than us. We all need support groups, church or whatever we choose. The idea is to have relationships in our recovery.

We must allow people to know us – to know our weaknesses. Oh! I forgot. We're too proud to allow that. Our pride will kill us! We'll find that being open and honest are rewarding; we can be set free from our bondage. When we run into trouble we need good healthy people in our network. If we don't, it may be too late.

It's the same with God. We have made many 911 calls; He has answered more times than anyone can imagine. We can make mistakes time and time again and get forgiveness. But there will come a day when it's too late for many. Jesus will say he never knew us. We knew who Jesus was, but we chose to not have a relationship with him.

It's imperative to have a relationship with God. This is the most important connection any one of us can ever have.

STEP 8

We have pain; we use unhealthy and wrong solutions to change the way we feel. We hurt ourselves and others and cause tremendous pain to those around us.

A lot of times we have these misconceived ideas that people in our lives have caused all our problems when maybe our manipulating didn't get us our way. We feel bitter and betrayed; we think we're being punished.

Even in recovery our perception of reality is often wrong. In recovery we're faced with all we have to do in Step 8. We have to make a list of those to whom we owe an apology. Did I hurt them or did they hurt me? Don't ponder; put them on your list.

The unknown is always scary. Will they accept my apology? I hate rejection. Remember, we have to do our part; we have to do the work. Some people will forgive us, some will accept us as we are and some will love us as they always have. These will be proud of us, support us and hope maybe this time will be different.

We know we will have to "reap what we sow." We have to deal with the consequences of our actions. We can't fool ourselves into thinking our deceptions will be forgotten. If we expect our apology to turn into a confrontation, we should not approach this person face to face. Another approach, perhaps a letter, would be better.

2 Corinthians 2:5-8 says that some will follow this advice and

accept your apology. We can't and shouldn't expect to be forgiven by all. These apologies are part of our recovery; they are as much for our benefit as they are for those we have wronged.

It may take time to cultivate forgiveness from others just as it takes time for us to recover. In time, when people see Christ in us, they will again want to be part of our lives.

When we confess to a person, it frees us; we are no longer bound. At this point forgiveness is on them, between them and God. It's like witnessing. I'm responsible for giving, not responsible if they don't receive it.

STEP 10

Step 10 is about continuing to take personal inventory and when wrong, promptly admitting it.

My attitude seems to get me in the most trouble mentally and spiritually. It makes a big difference in how I accept criticism, correction and discipline. Speaking of discipline, do I have any? Refer to Romans 7:18-20.

I know I'm rotten through and through as far as my old sinful nature is concerned. No matter which way I turn, I can't make myself do right. I want to, but I can't. When I want to do right, I don't. When I try not to do wrong, I do it anyway. But if I'm doing what I don't want to do, it's not I doing wrong but the sin in me.

Taking personal inventory is admitting my shortcomings. I need to look at myself, not others. The world teaches us to blame others, to look at their faults to better justify our own. We must take responsibility for our own minds and our own actions. We must do what is good, what is right. Tina says, "Just do the next right thing."

Romans 12:2 reads, "Do not be conformed to this world, but be transformed by the renewing of your mind, so that you may prove what the will of God is, that which is good, acceptable and perfect."

We have to take responsibility for our thoughts and our actions. When we have done wrong or wronged someone, promptly admit it. Ask for forgiveness and move on.

STRUGGLE

What is wrong with me? Why do I do the things I do? I have sobriety and the knowledge to make a sober life possible. From where do the temptations come? Why do I struggle?

The reason we have temptations and struggles is there was a time when addiction worked. Our bad behavior served a purpose at times and for a time. Even though we knew not to use drugs, we went ahead, knowing there would be consequences. We felt guilt and shame; we inflicted pain and despair on others. It still didn't matter.

If we were willing to throw everything away, there must have been something in it for us. We keep thinking drugs worked before. That's our twisted thinking. The very behavior we used to escape pain just caused more pain to ourselves and others. We struggle to stop this addictive behavior.

Look at how many things we can be addicted to besides alcohol and drugs; there's smoking, overeating and excess shopping to name a few. Anything we do excessively is addictive behavior. We even argue and fight regularly to always feel we are right and win at all costs. Could we have addictive personalities?

Many things can be considered addictive behavior. Just how many addictions can one person have? May I suggest all people have some sort of struggle. Addiction just multiplies and exaggerates it. Dysfunction is a learned behavior, acquired for survival.

When someone confronts us, we get defensive, blame them and make them the opposition; we play the victim. Even when things are going well, we have a tendency to create drama and chaos, because we are not comfortable just being still. This is the only way we know how to communicate and act.

We should look at all addictive behaviors for more than one reason. First we need to be aware of how many behaviors can be an addiction and can control our lives. These addictions can give a person their self-worth or help them project what they want the world to see. It keeps others from seeing inside, seeing the pain, fear, low self-esteem, etc.

Sacrifice is another behavior in which something is gained. Those who sacrifice only for self gratification or praise will never be fulfilled. They will always have an emptiness that can't be filled with worldly solutions. They will continue to struggle.

Our addictive behavior is illogical and normally gets unwanted results in the long haul. How do we change? We can change only by doing things differently. Biblically speaking, we must repent, turn around.

Insanity is doing the same things again and again expecting different results. Stop and think; then decide on a direction you want for your life.

Romans 7:22-23 says, "I love God's law with all my heart. But there is another law at work within me that is at war with my mind. This law wins the fight and makes me a slave to the sin that is still within me."

Webster says struggle is to make strenuous or violent efforts against opposition. Remember we must oppose the temptations of our sinful nature.

SUFFERING

It is understandable why our loved ones and others think addicts are cold hearted and only care for themselves. Addiction does cause us to be selfish, but it's a selfishness of the mind and not necessarily of the heart.

The truth is most of us are very sensitive, compassionate, loving people who never had any intention of hurting anyone. These traits actually are those which predisposition us to become addicts. Pain has a more devastating effect on us than the average person. We tend to take everything to heart; we think all problems are our fault whether we caused them or not. Our consciences will not allow us to do wrong without causing us more pain. Thus this causes the need for more relief (drugs) when we are in addiction.

Most of us are sincere when expressing concern to others when we recognize their pain, especially if we caused it. Unfortunately, our behavior does not convey the sincerity in our hearts. This is the behavior of addiction, not who we really are.

Our suffering makes us more compassionate to others. It helps us understand when someone is hurting and helps us know how to approach and comfort those in pain. No one can identify with pain like those of us who have lived through it, especially the pain of addiction.

It is necessary to suffer from time to time even in recovery; we do not need to get too comfortable during the good times. We have the need for others who have suffered from the grips of addiction to comfort us during hard times. When we allow support from others and give of ourselves willingly, we begin to understand how important relationships are to our well-being in recovery. We must stay connected.

Suffering is not meant to break us. It teaches us humility. It warns us of the consequences of our irresponsible behavior. It strengthens us and helps us develop good habits. Suffering is painful, but it promotes growth and maturity.

In recovery we will still have times of suffering. We can't make sense of why we should still suffer when we're doing well and making progress. We often question God as to why things happen to us. Did God intentionally cause this suffering? Is it punishment for our wrongdoings?

Why does God make or let us suffer? God never does anything to hurt us. He does give us free will to make decisions. When these decisions are bad or wrong ones, He allows us to suffer. At times there seems to be no reasonable explanation as to why. God expects us to trust his goodness regardless of what or when trouble arises in our lives. He can and will carry us through this trouble if we only trust Him.

Becoming a Christian is not a "get out of suffering" free card. When we run into hardships and trouble and hang tough, we illustrate a true unshakeable faith and trust in God. No matter what trials come our way, we must show our trust and know He is always in control. Suffering is, also, divine. God hurts when we do. God sent his son to earth to redeem humanity. Christ ultimately suffered an agonizing death for us.

Suffering purifies the heart. Suffering increases our hunger for God.

SURVIVAL

There were times I thought I wouldn't live to see another morning. How could one person consume the amount of drugs I had in one evening and live to see another day? I thought I'd probably go to sleep and not wake up.

When I opened my eyes the next morning and saw the sun peeking through the blinds, I could hardly believe I was still here. As I awoke through the fogginess, I wondered how my life became such a miserable mess. Angrily, I wondered why God was doing this to me.

I had survived yet another night and now had to face another day. I laid in bed with thoughts of being so afraid of living and dying alone. Was waking up my punishment for all I had done wrong? I never considered God had other plans for my life.

Realizing I had survived another night, I would attempt to make a commitment to the first minute and then the first hour. If I could just get through a day and make it to bed, maybe tomorrow would be a better day. I would pray to God to take me away from this miserable existence. Another day comes and the vicious circle begins again.

Have you ever prayed to God to help you now and you promise to never drink again as long as you live? Then after the sick hangover, we forget all too easily. We don't acknowledge that maybe God did help us out of that situation; we think we survived on our own. The fact is through stress, pressure, losses, tragedies, etc. we survived in spite of ourselves. There had to be a higher hand at work.

In the grips of active addiction, survival becomes a job. We develop techniques such as deceitful cons, creative manipulation and money juggling to name a few. We feel guilty and remorseful about some of the things we do, but we justify them as not being too bad. Eventually all our survival efforts and techniques seem to stop working; our luck runs out. We then decide our way doesn't work; eventually we have to depend on others for our survival.

In the beginning of recovery, we are taught to call someone when we are struggling. This works when we actually get in touch with the right person, but most of the time our pride kicks in and we find ourselves "white knuckling," holding on as tightly as we can; we're back in survival mode.

Along the way while looking for a way out, we cross paths with someone who realizes we need help. Perhaps they recognize their past behavior in us. My first intervention landed me in a secular, spiritual nonreligious program at a facility with a reputation as being the best. Well, as it turned out, the best was not good enough for me.

Secular programs are normally twelve step programs. Some of the steps were confusing to me; some I resented. I really disliked the idea of having to conform to a programmed way of life.

It has taken me three years to understand the difference between clean time and being sober. The secular programs teach us to count "one day at a time," and each and every day reminds us our identity will always relate to our past.

These programs are valid and have been proven time and time again to work. The fact is these steps were written in such a way as to lead people in the right direction so as not to offend anyone. The secular programs are necessary for those who think if there is a God, why is my life so miserable. The twelve steps actually will lead people to a god of their own understanding.

The program I chose as a last resort, given the fact I had out lived all expectations of medical technology and still had my health, was God's program. His is a one step program of repentance which erased all my past and gave me the freedom to live life to the fullest, to fulfill the purpose God has had in store for me.

God continues to send His angels to wake me morning after morning. Only God knew from the beginning for what I had been searching. I know now I only survived through the grace given to me by the one who sent His only begotten son to die for me. He saved me physically, mentally and spiritually.

"How grateful I am, and how I praise the Lord that you are concerned about me again. I know you have always been concerned for me, but for a while you didn't have the opportunity to help me" (Philippians 4:10).

Philippians 4:13 says, "For I can do everything with the help of Christ who gives me the strength I need."

"But even so, you have done well to share with me in my present difficulty" (Philippians 4:14).

"And this same God who takes care of me will supply all your needs from his glorious riches, which have been given to us in Christ Jesus" (Philippians 4:19).

TAKING FOR GRANTED

What do we take for granted? Everything! We are selfish, self-centered people who do nothing without expecting something in return. We think life is all about us. Everything from life's simplest pleasures to our greatest opportunities is taken for granted.

As Americans we have rights and freedoms. Perhaps the greatest of these is choice. We have the freedom to choose the direction our lives will take. We have the freedom to own a Bible and worship God.

We never stop to appreciate the basics of our lives, like waking up in the morning, taking a shower, getting dressed, eating breakfast, getting in the car and driving to work. Instead we gripe about the alarm going off, rush to get a quick shower, grab clothes that are not exactly what we want to wear, eat a granola bar instead of a big breakfast, get caught in traffic and hurry into work a little late. All this time we're thinking why does this always happen to me.

My wife tells her story like this. The alarm would go off at 5:00AM signaling the start of another dreaded day. Then she started working with two quadriplegic patients who quickly changed her attitude. These two men would have given anything to be able to turn off the alarm, get out of bed and take a shower unassisted, eat without having to be fed and walk to any job at all.

Even those incarcerated take their facilities and rights for granted. Think about being imprisoned in a foreign country where you would have no rights, being guilty until proven innocent, being ill-fed, beaten or raped. We take for granted the opportunities available in the system, such as GED classes, job skills, recovery classes and church. We have the freedom to be active and even smoke.

Who do we take for granted? For me, it's everyone who loves and cares for me. I take for granted all the unconditional things they do for me, the sacrifices they make. Think about the husband or wife who has worked or continues to work long and hard hours to keep the family together. Think about the mom or dad who has taken care of our bills during our addiction. Think about those children who have missed their childhood and been forced to grow up on their own. We even take our support groups for granted, those very people who reach out to us before and after things get out of hand.

The most important choice we have is to accept our Savior. In spite of our faults, God gives us grace. When we make bad choices, He gives forgiveness. In our ignorance God gives us wisdom. When we feel alone, He tells us He will never leave us or turn away from us. Yet we still go through life doing it our way and making a mess even though God can direct our steps.

When we want to give up and say we can't do it anymore, God says, "You can do all things" (Philippians 4:13). We say it won't be worth it; God says, "It will be worth it" (Romans 8:28). Just when we say we're tired of fighting, He says, "I will give you rest" (Matthew 11:28-30). We think it's impossible; God says, "All things are possible" (Luke 18:27). If we want to give up and say we're not able, God tells us we are (2 Corinthians 9:8).

I can't; He can. I choose to let Him.

God, thank you for your presence. Thank you for the large and small things in life we take for granted. Father, thank you for the quiet, the silence, the stillness when we can hear you, when we can honor and praise you, when we can be reminded that our life on earth is as close as we'll get to heaven without knowing you. We thank you for your protection, your mercy and grace even when we take you for granted. Everybody says, "Amen."

TERMS OF DENIAL

The majority of alcoholics and addicts are the last to admit to having a substance abuse problem, not to mention a life problem. We are not ignorant to the fact there is a problem; we're just confused as to the cause. By the time everyone realizes we have a problem, we can't see ourselves functioning without the drugs.

When confronted, we become defensive and even confrontational at times. Typically, most of us get irrational when the so-to-speak intervention begins or continues. Some of our most common responses are I don't have a problem, I've got it under control, I can stop anytime I want or since everyone thinks I am, I might as well.

Still in denial, if our addiction began with a prescription written by a physician, we justify our use because the doctor gave them to us. We say we need the drugs; our pain is so severe we can't live without them. This is one particular area in addiction where the addict is not necessarily lying or making excuses. Alcohol and drugs are mind altering; they change any and all reasonable thinking.

For the addict, this is the truth; we can't imagine life without the drugs. We have justified the use and misuse so long, we believe our own lies. Our own perception is the truth to us.

Any one of us who is deep into active addiction can not distinguish between what is real and what is not. We can not discern what is true or appropriate.

There comes a time when some of us have a moment of clarity and understand drugs have interrupted the normal course of our lives. We may, also, begin to realize drugs may not be the underlying cause of our problems.

Something happens and we find ourselves in need of recovery. It is difficult to understand our "pain" is the reason we sought a solution with drugs. So we certainly are confused in recovery when we go through even more suffering. Consequently, as a result most of us relapse.

With a small amount of recovery and knowing the right things to say, we approach people and tell them how well we're doing. This is often followed by some sympathetic reason why we're broke and need money or some kind of help. The truth is when we're well and doing well in recovery, we don't need to tell anyone; it's obvious.

The people who have been our support and accountability group usually recognize our behavior before we relapse. These people would rather us be honest with them. When we're in trouble, we need to go to them and ask for help. Denial hurts everyone – us and them.

"Therefore God also gave them up to uncleanness, in the lusts of their hearts, to dishonor their bodies among themselves, who exchanged the truth of God for the lie, and worshipped and served the creature rather than the Creator, who is blessed forever" (Romans 1:24-25).

TOLERANCE

When we think of the word tolerance, are we thinking about people or circumstances? The traditional definition of tolerance is to recognize and respect others' beliefs, opinions and behaviors without agreeing or sympathizing with them. Most people believe everyone has the right to their opinion.

Society has created a new age definition. It says all beliefs are equally valid and everyone should be tolerant to all new ideas. It considers every person as individual and each one has the right to their own morals, values and lifestyles. Society says not only should we respect their beliefs but should accept their behaviors, also.

Why have we become tolerant? Have we been taught to be passive or to be non-judgmental? Are we really that patient? Do we know how to use discernment and understanding or do we just accept whatever? Have we become conformed by this world?

As addicts our addictions have transformed us. We have programmed ourselves to tolerate anything and everything. Don't rock the boat! My comfort zone is null and void. Avoid confrontation at all costs. Even when we can distinguish between right and wrong, our guilt won't allow us to stand up. We just tolerate whatever comes along so we won't be involved.

On the other hand, let us get clean for a little while and all hell breaks loose. We get defensive and rebellious. We are confused about the things we should and need to tolerate.

In recovery sometimes we meet different personalities we can't tolerate. We have little tolerance for people who point out our shortcomings and seem to belittle us. Then we have the programs with all their mottos and clichés. They almost force the theory addiction is a disease. My addiction progressed to the point I didn't even like myself, not to mention the people trying to tell me how to live.

I think we are confused about what we should and should not tolerate. We have to tolerate the fact we may not ever be accepted by some. If we want to recover, we should reevaluate the things we can and can't tolerate. Hold on to good morals, values and beliefs and change the way we think.

We do have the right to question and evaluate all teachings, to agree or disagree, not about who is right or wrong but what is right or wrong. Make a commitment to stand up for the truth. Never justify it or you'll compromise your morals and beliefs.

My wife told me a story about a frog. If you put a frog into a pot of boiling water, he'll hop out. But if you place him in a pot of lukewarm water and then turn on the heat, he'll tolerate it until it kills him.

"If another person falls into sin, you who are godly should gently and humbly help that person back into the right path. Be careful not to fall into the same temptation yourself. Share each other's troubles and problems, and in this way obey the law of Christ" (Galatians 6:1-2).

"Let us live in love and be a witness for the truth of God"

TOTAL COMMITMENT

After living in a very selfish world where we only thought of ourselves and our wants and needs, we recovering alcoholics have a tremendous amount of changing to do. This change is for our own sake and recovery and the sake of our families and friends.

There has to come a point in our lives where we become so empty, literally hating life as it is, that we are willing to make a total commitment to overcoming addiction. In recovery we have a chance to begin a new life. We must commit to responsibility. It will be apparent to those around us if we're too lazy to do the work. Expecting others to take care of us will normally lead to failure. This is our recovery; we are responsible for it.

In our recovery programs, there are suggestions that are offered for our own good. There are guidelines and rules that are required of us; these have been successfully used by many in recovery. If we are accountable for all our actions, both past and future, and show the willingness and determination to recover, hopefully we can regain trust and become a responsible and productive member of society once again.

The chance we have at a new way of life is totally up to us and us alone. No one who hasn't walked in these shoes can understand this. Each one of us individually has a responsibility to make good healthy moral choices and decisions. We do this by making plans and setting goals.

We should always consider the feelings and needs of those who support us. We must be very careful that in desperation we don't use and manipulate people when our expectations are unreasonable. Of course, we must think of what is best for us, but what is best for us should never be at someone else's cost. Remember to "not hurt anyone today."

Beware of becoming bored or depressed which are repercussions of laziness. Finding new people, places and activities can be uncomfortable at times. It may be hard to fit in or find anything in common.

Recovery is the common ground. Consider the worst day in recovery is better than any day that was controlled by addiction. We have to deny our wants and desires. We must be willing to set aside our own agenda in favor of finding complete gratification from everything we do. We must commit whole heartedly to facing discomfort in dealing with our past and embarrassment facing those we have wronged.

When our primary goal is change and we continue to try new ways, unfamiliar becomes familiar and uncomfortable becomes comfortable. Then challenges become fun. Being partially committed usually ends in less than desirable results and eventually failure. We must be totally committed.

Relationships are our number one reason for relapse. We must pursue a total unselfish commitment to recovery and each other to survive addiction. One can not be strong for both. We should not let our relationships hold us back. We need to be aware of and careful of our association with weak people. Their example alone and trying to carry them will make us weak.

In Luke 14, Jesus says we cannot be inconsistent, ungrateful or half-hearted and be a true child of God. He says, "He cannot be my disciple." God says we must be totally committed to him. Deuteronomy 6:5 says, "Love God with all your heart, soul, and mind."

Luke 14, also, speaks of loving God first, over and above all relationships. It says anyone who wants to follow him must hate his own life, meaning to be willing to put down everything in order to fulfill his purpose for you and find life as in his promises. What He gives us in return is beyond value!

"If anyone desires to come after me, let him deny himself and take up his cross and follow me" (Matthew 16:24). We have to be totally committed to be his disciple.

TRADING PLACES

It's important to replace our old addictive lives with healthy thoughts and activities. We as addicts and alcoholics will always have addictive personalities. We will always be going ninety to nothing with our hair on fire. For us, it's all or nothing.

We have to accept and accommodate our addictive personalities. In the beginning of recovery, we may need to become obsessed with a healthy alternative, such as getting fit physically. Choose something that takes your mind off the drugs and alcohol.

Most of us live two separate lives. There is the functional one where we're successful at school, work and civic activities. This is the side the world knows and loves – the kind hearted, honest and basically good old boy. Then there is the other life – a life of lying, cheating, thieving. This despicable person is living a life of deception.

We live in fear of being caught, but as time passes we develop a tremendous amount of arrogance. We've gotten away with it this long. We won't get caught.

Inevitably, there is a collision; our behavior alone gives us up. People get tired of being lied to. The deceit closes in. There is a serious train wreck on the horizon. My dad once said to me, "When things get bad, they usually get worse before they get better." Normally we have to exhaust every means and all resources before hitting bottom.

Consequences are what they are but usually don't stop us. If they did, the first time we were confronted or lost a job or relationship or were arrested, we would stop. We have to become completely empty before we can rise up again.

God in His infinite wisdom, being the beginning and the end, has an unique way of protecting us from complete destruction. While giving us free will, He knows exactly what He is doing, what we are doing and what He has planned for our lives.

It is our choice to continue our destructive ways or to follow Him. It is our decision to be discontented or to accept His grace, love and mercy for us. Jeremiah 29:11 says, "For I know the plans I have for you. They are plans for good and not disaster, to give you a future and hope." It continues to say when you pray, He will listen. When you look for Him whole-heartedly, He will be found. He will end your captivity and restore your fortunes. And He will bring us, the lost, home again.

We are learning to slow down and let life happen. We know there are certain things beyond our control. We are beginning to be thankful for what we have and are finding a peace and joy in our lives. We can feel a sense of relief to not be where we once were. This feeling of freedom cannot be explained.

Trading places? Are you willing to do what it takes to stay sober and make your life complete? Are you willing to do your part, stop being lazy at recovery, stop giving up? The easy way is to just return to the misery.

I had a conversation with a friend about becoming and living as a Christian. He laughed and said, "The hard choice is usually the right choice."

Nothing valuable in life comes easy; it comes at a cost. But if it's worth having, it's worth working for.

Eternal life is free for the asking. All we have to do is give up our selfish ways and follow Jesus. In Acts 5, Ananias and Sapphira sold some land and gave part of the money to the Apostles, claiming to have given them the full amount. Their sins led to instant death. Now we are all guilty of lies and half-truths. These may not lead to our deaths but will eventually cause us to fail in recovery.

There is a time for all of us to trade places and seek new goals in life. Recovery involves letting go of the past, holding on to the present and building a new life for the future.

THE TRAP

Studies show about 13 million Americans have an alcohol/substance disorder. An estimated 10% of any given community has an abuse problem. These figures may be underestimated. A huge majority of women go undetected. Normally women are non-confrontational; therefore their abuse gains very little attention.

Men represent the greater percentage of the statistics. Women represent the higher percentage of those addicted to prescription medications. Young adults between eighteen and twenty-nine tend to be the highest alcohol abusers.

The highest number of abusers is functional adults who maintain jobs, have a family life, participate in civic activities and events and even attend church. Most appear to have normal lives.

Some studies say there are two kinds of substance disorders: abuse and addiction. ABC says the four stages are use, misuse, abuse and dependency. Use is occasional, misuse gets drunk on occasion, abuse gets drunk every time and dependency has to have the substance in order to function.

Addiction, also, has a pattern: (1)experimental, (2)social or recreational, (3)using to change moods or change the way we feel and/or (4)psychological dependency. ABC describes mental and/or emotional pain as the reason for the beginning of addiction.

There are many excuses or triggers for our use. Learned behavior (family history, lifestyles, peers), stress and some psychological disorders cause excessive abuse. The drugs give a false sense of the solution to our pain and problems and for a short time some sort of feeling normal.

In dealing with addiction, our behavior typically runs anywhere from denial, anger, fear, frustration to guilt. We get annoyed easily when we are questioned; we use our anger in an attempt to control other people's response to our behavior. We, also, avoid the responsibility of recovery with this same behavior.

Here is the "trap." Addiction is very cunning. In the beginning drugs work for us, at least for a short while. Yet the pain is still there when we come down from our high. We use more and more drugs until our brains become immune to the substance. See the drugs have stopped working, but the consequences are compounded. We have developed an addiction and cannot function without the drugs.

Addiction is a family problem; therefore recovery must be a combined focus for the family. Individuals, companions and families may have to change their habits, patterns, lifestyles and beliefs. It is important that everyone involved is considerate to each other's feelings and make a conscientious effort to make healthy decisions. If, by chance, family members are unwilling to support change or are codependent and will jeopardize recovery, the addict must find a way to cope and maybe learn how to love from a distance.

In Romans 8:28, we read, "We know that all things work together for good to those who love God, to those who are called according to his purpose."

Proverbs 23 speaks of our addictions leading to loss, the loss of reputation, marriage, family, job, home, etc. Verses 20 and 21 say, "Do not carouse with drunkards and gluttons for they are on their way to poverty." Furthermore, the verses say our laziness will clothe us in rags.

Daniel 5 tells the story of how Belshazzar and his officials, in their drunkenness, were defenseless and the Babylonian Empire was captured. During our addiction we are, also, defenseless. We try to justify our problems and continue to make a mess.

In recovery we have the problem of becoming even more defenseless. But sobriety offers the opportunity to get honest, see our mess and manage our dysfunction rather than repair our damage and recover our losses. In the beginning of recovery, we can only see how messed up we are; it's hard to see hope for the future.

The journey to recovery is worth it! We may or may not have lost a lot during our addiction, but those who surrender to God and live for Him get a freedom and peace that can never be lost.

UNCOMFORTABLE SILENCE

Have you ever know anyone who could not be satisfied with anything? They can't be still; they always have to be doing something. Can we as addicts relate to this behavior? We can recognize this behavior in others, but if we take a honest look at ourselves, this describes us.

There is a personality type identified as the achiever. This person always has the need to accomplish some task. Being productive is necessary for their self-satisfaction and well being. Some people just enjoy challenges and enjoy completing projects. Then there are those who work for the praise they will receive for a completed task.

Many times the achiever gets caught up in the compulsion and the joy fades away. He becomes obsessed with getting the job done, finishing it right away; it's like fighting fire. The achiever has very high expectations for himself and many times has the same for others. He expects everyone to carry his own weight and doesn't understand why everyone is not as productive as he.

Then there is the achiever who has a performance oriented personality; he has to do it all himself. Yet, at times, he'll get in a situation where time is running out, and he'll get irritated when no one pitches in to help. This behavior, also, shows up when the achiever has a dominate personality; he has control issues.

The behavior of most of us addicts is the constant rearranging or fixing all aspects of our lives on the outside. Nothing seems to be in the right place. No one understands. We have been known to rearrange the furniture, clean when nothing is dirty, buy everything new, trade cars or change clothes several times. Nothing seems comfortable; things just don't feel right.

If we could only grasp the fact the problem may not be on the outside; the people and things in our lives may not be the problem. When we can come to grips with getting the inside right, everything on the outside will come together and fit just fine. Even if everything isn't perfect, we can be content and truly satisfied with how and where we are.

In any addiction known to man, there is a void people are trying to fill. Our desire to find peace in the silence causes us to seek for it in many ways. Using drugs to change the way we feel was our way of a search for God. At first experience the drugs seemed like heaven, but no one gets to heaven by changing the external. We can't find heaven without changing the internal.

If we allow Jesus to be with us in our discomfort when we are coming apart, when the storms are out-of-control and the fires are burning, God will grant us peace. We can attain the peace for which we are searching only if God is by our side.

In Mark 4:39, Jesus is saying to us to just believe in our hearts that He can settle the storms. "Peace, be still and the winds died down and became perfectly calm."

In Luke 10:38, we read about the Martha and Mary who were both followers of Jesus. Martha was an achiever, conscientious and always concerned with details of how things looked. She was adamant to the point of criticizing Mary for not helping. Mary, on the other hand, was very devoted to Christ. She was extremely aware of his presence, dedicated to spending quiet time, treasured sitting at his feet and listening to his voice. Which follower had more peace?

When we are too busy getting things done, even good things, and miss spending time with Jesus, our growth in recovery will be slower and more painful. Allowing Jesus to go with us through difficult times will help us to grow in strength and in faith. Only then can we enjoy the silence.

THE VICTIM

It's not my fault; it wasn't me. I don't know anything about it. Somebody cheated me. Nothing ever works out my way! If it wasn't for that cop, I wouldn't be in trouble. I'm the victim here!

Webster says a victim is a person who suffers or a person destroyed through no fault of his own. Secular programs say the alcoholic/addict is the victim of some event or time in his life that created a tremendous amount of pain.

Addiction begins when the "victim" discovers a solution to his pain. As addicts progress and become dependent, they become crippled not only by the drugs but by "playing the victim."

There is the possibility of learned behavior; everything from my parents did it to everyone in my neighbor does it to it's the only way I know to live. Then there is the codependent person in our lives who gives us the perfect excuse; that poor baby was in the wrong place at the wrong time or he was singled out or he was with the wrong crowd.

Being the victim, the user holds guilt over the heads of the people who love and try to help and protect him. The addict uses guilt to justify his actions.

The addict gets comfortable playing the victim. This is dangerous because he loses all desire and ability to change his circumstances.

234

Continuing to blame others leads to laziness. He refuses to accept responsibility for his actions.

Recovery says I can no longer be a victim. I must take responsibility for my actions. I must stop making excuses. Dr. Phil McGraw says you can't change what you don't acknowledge. Get real with yourself about your life. If you are unwilling to acknowledge your behavior, thoughts, problems and circumstances, then you cannot and will not change.

As we refuse to recognize our own self-destructive behaviors, they continue, gain momentum and eventually become so engrained, we become more and more resistant to change. If we think we reap some kind of benefit from denying our behavior is a problem, we are not being honest with ourselves.

We cannot afford to be defensive, tell lies and be in denial. Denial kills all hopes and dreams for the future. It will compromise any chance for recovery. We can play the victim and continue a miserable existence or literally die from denial, or we can choose to recover.

I'm not saying this will be easy. To recover will take hard work. You must examine your part in every situation. It's not your responsibility for what happened; it is your responsibility to recognize your part and recover from it.

"For whatever is born of God overcomes the world; and this is the victory that has overcome the world" (1 John 5:4).

We are targeted victims of Satan. The good news is Satan only has the power we give him. Have faith and trust in God, and together we will overcome.

WEAKNESS

Pain is a part of living. But for some, pain is a way of life; their pain is constant. Whether our pain is physical, mental or emotional, it drains us of energy and even causes confusion. We become hopeless at times, even suicidal.

All the physical weaknesses and the negative mental and emotional thoughts disconnect us from our relationships with our families and our loving God. They, also, rob us of our motivation.

Clinical studies have shown that depression causes pain to worsen. Our attitudes change, temptations get stronger and our control weakens. We find ourselves in a deep depression; we can't laugh or cry. We get irritable and act out or react wrongly to situations because we have lost our ability to be still and reason with our emotions. When we get stressed out, we have a tendency to get angry about the smallest of things. Our tempers get out-of-hand, and we get out-of-control.

When pain has become intolerable, we want to change the way we feel. Now we are faced with the fight or flight syndrome. We must always have a plan of action for dealing with the times we are the weakest.

There are programs, group meetings, church and Bible studies for people fighting the same weaknesses we have. There are activities in which we can become involved to help with our struggles. We can start a hobby, exercise, get reacquainted with family and friends and stay connected with a network of service oriented groups.

Remember the acrostic for JOY: always put 'J'esus first, 'o'thers next and 'y'ourself last. I learned this is what you do to fight depression: get off the couch, turn off the TV, close the door behind you, go across the street and help someone.

The reason for activities and staying connected is to keep focused on recovery and not on the problem. Busy work keeps our minds from concentrating on what could have been and keeps us focused on the task ahead.

At the same time we have to be cautious about the possibility of doing too much, getting too much on our plates and getting so tired it takes our focus off recovery. We have become so accustomed to using drugs to alter our performance, to give us energy or to slow us down. When we get sober we normally feel better and have the potential to overdo it. If we physically hurt ourselves, we now have a body and mind problem – a body with physical pain and a mind that obsesses over the wrong solution for the pain.

Using and feeling no physical pain can disable us and lead to death because of our inability to respond to fatigue or injury. Pain and weakness are warnings for what is dangerous. Our physical health is vital to our mental and emotional well being. Our conscience can warn us of evil dangers and moral troubles. Fear is a healthy emotion that makes us sensitive to risky situations.

Pain causes desperation. In our desperate state we become lost. When all our efforts have failed, our last resort is to look to God. Somewhere along the way we've lost sight of Him; now in our weakness He shows himself to us. Pain creates the potential to deepen our faith and mature our spiritual strength and wisdom so we become more like Christ.

"And he said unto me, my grace is sufficient for you, for my strength is made perfect in weakness" (2 Corinthians 12:9). A literal translation is I am glad to boast about my weaknesses, so the power of Christ may work through me.

John 16:33 reads, "I have told you all this so that you may have peace in me. Here on earth you will have many trials and sorrows. But take heart, because I have overcome the world."

WHAT IS RECOVERY?

A majority of society has the impression that recovery is "getting off drugs." Getting off the substance is only a small part, although it's the key, in recovery. Addicted people can have abstinence from drugs and still have underlying causes that led to their drug use and dependent behavior.

There are many detoxification programs in place. These programs work the medical aspect; they handle physical withdrawals and some of the mental cravings.

There are many different rehabilitation programs where the addict and his family can receive help for addiction. These programs teach some sort of structure through exercise, diet, relaxation techniques, social skills and counseling.

The choices of the programs are secular or Christian or a combination of the two. The different programs give an individual the options in order to recover. The various programs, also, deal with all types of dysfunction from sexual, overeating, alcohol, drugs, etc.

Many family members will say, "I just want him back.' They believe if he could just get off drugs, he would be his old self again. Normally, this is not true. After a person has become dependent on drugs, their attitude and personality change. Extended use causes a person to display behavior he would never have displayed otherwise.

At first drugs give a person comfort, relief and a sense of security.

As drug use becomes an addiction, the drugs cause more pain. The addict starts to build resentment and blames the pain on whomever is a good target. All this time the drugs are actually contributing to his pain. The addict hurts or destroys relationships and manipulates people and situations. Attempts at intervention cause the addict to get paranoid and to isolate himself. Only when the addict realizes the drugs have stopped working and are actually working against him and when it's evident drugs have caused enough pain can he be ready to commit to a recovery program.

The process of recovery for the addict is to get clean and secondly to realize the drugs themselves are not his only problem. Then each individual is analyzed so there is a clean and clear view of what happened and the consequences created.

In some programs, the drugs are seen as just a symptom of some underlying problem. What kind of problem? It can be anything that has caused unbearable pain from possibly childhood though adulthood. These range from family problems, divorce, violence, cruel punishment, peer pressure, self-esteem, etc. The pain has to be identified.

From what was the addict trying to escape? Identify the pain, examine it and forgive! He isn't responsible for that pain or for what caused it. He is responsible for his recovery.

The addict has already suffered and endured much pain getting to this point. Recovery will not be comfortable; it will be painful at times. He has to ask and give forgiveness to all he has hurt or who he thinks hurt him. He must look at his past and make restitution whenever and wherever possible. Before acting, he must always make sure his intentions are good.

At this point, the addict has a back seat view of just how drugs have created a different character and personality. The addict must be committed to change. Dedication to recovery will show family and friends he has a desire to change.

Recovery requires help.

Recovery requires change; it requires willingness.

Recovery requires honesty and integrity,

Recovery requires action.

Recovery is not arrogant and is open to learning.

Recovery is not selfish; it gives as much as it receives.

Most of all, recovery requires God!

Come to believe and allow God, through his son Jesus Christ, to give you true peace and freedom. God gives us the tools to achieve what we thought was impossible. Relationships can be restored; we can have joy. Our joy reaches out and translates to happiness and contentment. Recovery is not for the addict alone. Everyone around him benefits and deserves this peace.

"The spirit of the Lord God is upon me, because the Lord has anointed me to bring the good news to the afflicted; he has sent me to bind up the broken-hearted, to proclaim liberty to captives and freedom to prisoners" (Isaiah 61:1).

WHAT NOW!

When I began to wonder what I was going to do now, someone said sacrifice. Since living in active addiction for so much of my life, sacrifice on my part was not something I knew. Addiction sacrifices nothing for anyone.

Of course, plenty of people have sacrificed for me over the years. I'm sure you've had people sacrifice for you, too. Fact is some have sacrificed until we've used them up or until they realized we didn't appreciate them.

We may think we've sacrificed since we went to work today or went to a school function or a family get-together. Maybe you went to church. In the back of your mind, did you have the idea that now somebody owes you something in return? You haven't sacrificed anything for anyone.

A meaningful sacrifice is giving up your wants for the benefit of another. To sacrifice is to give, to give up something for which you care. Giving something that means nothing to you is not a sacrifice.

You must have something in order to sacrifice it. We all have time and talents. We can take the time and do something for someone else. We can use our talents for the good of others; we can give back to society.

In recovery, my best talent was making coffee. I sacrificed my time by getting there early and making the coffee. I, also, shared my heart and my tears. Sharing was a sacrifice for me. This sharing helped others as well as me.

When I think of my recovery, I have to consider all those I've hurt. I may have to sacrifice my own feelings for a time to allow loved ones to openly share the hurt I've caused them; they're working toward their recovery.

I may have to sacrifice my authority for a while. In active addiction, I forced my children to assume authority. Now I need to win/gain this authority back at their pace.

To sacrifice is no more me first. Hebrews 13:16 reads, "Do not neglect doing good and sharing, for with such sacrifices God is pleased."

The sacrifice most important to recovery and to salvation is self. "I beg you therefore, brethren, by the mercies of God, that you present your bodies a living sacrifice, holy and acceptable unto God" (Romans 12:1).

WHO AM I?

Early in my recovery I was asked, "Who are you?" My answer was Delno Jones. "Wrong," he said. "That's your name. Who are you?" "I'm a hairdresser." "Wrong, that's what you do, your profession. Who are you?" Trying to concentrate, I struggled to find the right answer. "I'm a failure, a screw-up." "Wrong, that's what happened to you. Who are you?" By now I was getting frustrated, actually mad; I gritted my teeth and blurted out, "I'm a drug addict."

Honestly, I'm still not sure what that particular counselor was expecting or wanted my response to be. I do know he made the assessment that I didn't think very highly of myself. The programs teach us to simply identify ourselves as addicts.

In addiction we tend to lose our identity. Initially, we find some sort of creative thinking during our use of drugs. This thinking is nothing but delusional, clouded, irrational thoughts; this is not reality. Even so, the more we use, the less of this false creativity and motivation we have. We become an empty shell. We become what society thinks we are.

So, now, who am I? My favorite uncle, Paul, once said to me, "You can make a reputation for yourself in a short while that will take a lifetime to live down." He was right! I made this reputation for myself that allows people to identify me as being a drug addict. I believed it, too.

Society, also, identifies us by the mistakes we have made and the seemingly immoral acts and decisions drug addiction has made for us. It's my job to relate to you and help you understand that you under normal conditions would not have done these things, but addiction will make you. None of us ever set out to hurt people. However, we have to take responsibility for our actions whether addiction caused them or not.

In recovery the process of undoing the past is virtually impossible. What is possible is making good, healthy choices today and in the future so we can start believing in ourselves and living a better life, clean and sober.

So how do we do this? One day at a time! We need to recognize our wrongs and admit to our shortcomings. Mainly, we need to get rid of our selfish behavior. Recovery is then obtainable.

Whether in addiction or recovery, when we feel trapped, we need to ask ourselves who am I in Christ? Most of us have the misconception that God is judgmental as we are. We have a vision of a man sitting in heaven taking notes of every dysfunctional and devious thing we've ever done. We think we can never right our wrongs.

We're wrong! God is an ever forgiving God, a God of love. Nothing we can ever do will take away God's love for us.

In the past, we lived a life of so called excitement, mystery and danger. Recovery can seem boring. It's because we still have the inability to accept delayed gratification. Galatians 6:9 says, "So don't get tired of doing what is good. Don't get discouraged and give up for we will reap the harvest of blessing at the appropriate time."

The writer Paul says we will reap what we sow. Our addiction has brought about painful consequences for us and others. God tells us to change from our behavior, to repent. He tells us to stop struggling to have our own needs met and to minister to the needs of others.

Using God's word as a standard way of life will be apparent through our actions. When we begin to understand who God is and we become a follower of Jesus Christ, we will begin to develop his character - his love, patience, joy, kindness, gentleness, self-control and peace. When we act in the spirit of God, our actions will speak for themselves.

Jesus asked in Matthew 16:15, "Who do you say I am?" Simon Peter answered, "You are the Christ, the son of the living God."

So who am I? Christ is in me. I am a child of God. I, too, am a son of God. I have a new identity!

Life begins when we discover who we are. Matthew 16:25 says, "For whoever wishes to save his life will lose it, for whoever loses his life for my sake will find it."

WORTHY – HAVING MERIT

Are we worthy? We don't feel very worthy; at least I didn't for a long time. I do believe it's possible for addicts to become worthy again.

When we get a job, we can get there early, be dependable, work hard, have a good attitude, help others, be humble, accept correction and constructive criticism, don't complain and do a good day's work. Then we'll be worthy of working for this company. We'll be blessed to have a job when others are not so lucky.

We should be faithful in attending our recovery meetings. When we go, we should go with a good attitude and an open mind, be tolerate (not critical) of others, offer help when we can, be humble, accept correction and constructive criticism, share our hopes and dreams, ask for advice if needed and give advice when appropriate. We should ask God to guide and direct us. We will grow and mature and be worthy of being in recovery.

We can be worthy in our relationships by being honest and true. When we come clean and tell the whole truth, we've done the right thing. When we have respect for our fellow man, we become worthy of his friendship. When we serve our fellow man, we create lasting relationships. When we can give and expect nothing in return, we become worthy.

What does it take to be worthy of our children? We have a tendency to fall into the past and feel overwhelmed by guilt. Don't! Try to let it go. Accept the fact that nothing can be done about yesterday.

Today is a new day; hold your head up and be a good example. If you make a promise, keep it; we've broken enough. Be careful not to make promises you can't keep. We desperately want to make up for our past disappointments. We have to be careful not to set ourselves up for failure.

Be a good leader to your children. Redirect their paths; we have to try to break the cycle of learned behavior. Your actions will speak louder than words. Be there and be sober.

We, also, need to give our children time to give the responsibility and authority of parenthood back to us. Some of us have forced our children to be the adults, to be the parents in our families. We need to earn our rights as parents back. Be patient. Children want and need good, healthy parents. Children are resilient. They in time will come back to us.

Let us be worthy of our church. Here we can develop the healthiest of relationships. Don't be discouraged by the so called Christians who talk about us, look down their noses at us and think we don't belong in church. Go to church for the right reason, to be one with God. Go to church to learn more about God and to praise him.

We should be diligent about our recovery; real Christians will want to be part of this. What a witness we can be to others! We become worthy of our church when we give back what has been given to us. Good things come to those who give of themselves. God has a place for us in church.

Let us live a life that is worthy of God. None of us are really worthy of his grace, but He's always there for all of us. When things are going well for us, we may forget where we've been. We may take God and his goodness for granted. We may quit working toward becoming all that God wants us to be. Let us not forget – except for the grace of God, we might be here at all!

Matthew 10:10 tells us the worker is worthy of God's support. We need not worry about an abundance; God's support is enough.

Luke 10:7 says, "For the laborer is worthy of his wages."

"Only conduct yourself in a manner worthy of the gospel of Christ, so that whether I come and see you or remain absent, I will hear of you that you are standing firm in one spirit, with one mind striving together for the faith of the gospel" (Philippians 1:27).

When we come to God broken and He clothes us with his righteousness, then we become worthy of salvation. Salvation comes only from God.

God bless you.

ENDORSEMENTS

After years of reading endorsements, it surprises me that I would be asked to be an endorser. I feel so inadequate in my own walk that being asked to endorse another's work is humbling and, in some ways, intellectually and emotionally overwhelming.

I have been pursuing a career as a psychotherapist for over 17 years now, and most of the time feeling I have just begun. The whole idea that we feel or think we understand the motivation of another is somewhat arrogant and unloving. It is easy to make assumptions about another's thoughts, allowing us to place our own self-serving morals, values and judgment on them.

This brings me to Mr. Jones, Delno as he is better known. He is a master of acceptance. For over 45 years I have been amazed at the level of love and compassion one human can demonstrate. I have observed for years his ability for true unselfish love.

Several years ago Delno shared that he was writing with heart felt brutal honesty a series of stories about compassion, love, caring and sharing. It has been my pleasure, at times, to read various parts of his stories, only to be amazed at the depth a "Hair Dresser" without formal training could relay to the reader. I must confess that maybe, just maybe, it is another observation of divine influence. Maybe Delno is truly one of the chosen few who is and continues to be inspired by our Lord and Savior.

I really believe Delno has "fought" his way to discover the "secret."

The secret is true love, which passes all understanding. He has a heart that only sees the best in others and the things they have to offer to all of us. If you are ever in his presence, you will never forget him with those piercing blue eyes that only God could be hiding behind. He has a smile that assures you all is well.

I hope you get a chance to stand with this man someday. If not, read his words and feel the presence of God and be encouraged by one of his earthly angels.

I will never fully understand humanity but will continue to search for truths. I am grateful to men like Delno who give me hope, challenge me, provoke thought and has taught me the value of unconditional love.

Sincerely,
vJoseph F. (Joey) Smith, MA, LPC

As you journey through these pages, if you have ever struggled with addiction in any capacity either as an addict or through a relationship, you will know that the author has walked in your shoes. This is a sincerely personal and honest sharing of the addict's world with the reader's journey consistently benefiting from scriptural support.

Tom Caldwell, PhD

This is one of the most valuable books written on recovery. It was not birthed in a clinic by a team of doctors. This is a compilation straight from the heart of a former addict who has experienced the personal struggles of the fight to freedom. After reading this book every addict and those close to an addict can know that victory is possible. As a personal devotional or as a guideline for group study, this book will help you secure hope for a bright and better future.

Robert, a former addict loved by Jesus

This book, a collection of papers, by Delno Jones, a respected citizen of our little town, owner of a local beauty shop and close friend, has been used by him in classes for inmates suffering from alcohol and drug addiction at a nearby penal institution. The advice he gives these addicts and his own touching confessions about his struggles and his return to a normal productive life are extremely effective. Delno has empathy for these inmates; he has been in their shoes.

He talks about feelings of guilt, inferiority, insecurity, anger, denial, complacency and problems of identity. He says the only way to a normal healthy living is repentance and acceptance of Jesus Christ.

Is this book only useful to addicts? I definitely doubt that. We all fall short of the glory of God. We need to be humble and repentant. To different degrees and in different ways, we all struggle. This is good reading for everyone.

Franz Eitel, PhD

Hopelessly addicted to hydrocodone and cocaine, Delno entered treatment at Victory Home in Tallulah Falls, Georgia, on January 29, 2007. He had experienced brief moments of sobriety through 12-step programs and counseling, but his on-going bondage to drugs kept him in misery. Twenty weeks later he graduated from Victory Home, a new man in Christ and free from addiction. Since then he has actively been involved in prison and recovery ministries and now serves on the Board of Directors of Victory Home. Spending precious moments with Christ and reflecting daily on his recovery, Delno blesses us by sharing his thoughts in writing. I pray that you will find his reflections insightful and encouraging as you, too, seek the abundant life that only Jesus Christ can provide.

Rev. Richard A. Pletsch, M.Div., M.A.C.M.
Executive Director of Victory Home – Helping Hand, Inc.

www.ingramcontent.com/pod-product-compliance
Lightning Source LLC
Chambersburg PA
CBHW030256290526
45785CB00001B/106